Mary's Miracles and Messages

- a True Story of a Visionary's Journey

by Claire Papin

Foreword by Catherine Lanigan

Lighted Paths
www.LightedPaths.org

ISBN: 978-1-61750-815-8

Edited by Sandy Penny
www.SandyPenny.com

Lighted Paths
www.LightedPaths.org

DEDICATION

This book is dedicated to Mother Mary, who has been a nurturing guide to me through much of my journey. To my mother Phyllis, my other mother Carole Dean, my beloved Robert, and my dear friends Sandy Penny, Catherine Lanigan, and Elizabeth Best … all of whom believed in me and the importance of sharing my heart and experiences.

Contents

FOREWORD

I met Claire Papin nearly twenty-five years ago, just about the time she received her first visitation from Mother Mary. At the same time, my father was given a profound divine directive for me during his Near Death Experience. A "Being of Light" told my father that I was to write books in which I chronicled "peoples' interaction with angels." These two life-altering experiences not only aided in the bond between Claire and me, but have continued to keep our minds, hearts and souls in a loving friendship all these years. Often we find ourselves thinking of one another at exactly the same time, and usually about the same subject.

I was a guest several times on Claire's radio programs for both Wisdom Radio and Lime Radio when she was living in Houston. Claire was and is one of those gentle, loving and compassionate souls that I believe God so wisely chooses to communicate His messages and His love to humanity and the earth.

Claire's stories have always fascinated me and she has generously allowed me to share them in my third book about angels, miracles and signs, *Angel Tales*. Her own book, *"Mary's Miracles and Messages – a True Story of a Visionary's Journey"* is eloquently written with a dusting of wisdom from some of the great spiritual minds and visionaries of the past and our contemporary age.

For over two and a half decades, Claire must have felt at times that she was a "voice crying out in the wilderness." However, she has never once wavered in her deep and steely faith in the goodness of man, and her own hope for a glorious new world that is quickly manifesting for us all. Despite the chaos and seemingly dire times in which we live, human beings are truly evolving and our energies are being elevated to a new frequency. The Veil between the dimensions is being thinned and the "visions" that Claire and others "see" will become more of the norm and not the exception in the decades to come. Mother Mary's prediction, through Claire, is that peace will prevail. It is in that sacred space of peace and love, where we will find grace and the understanding that we are all One. There is no separation between man and God.

And no separation between the earth and man.

In every word that Claire writes, her passion for mankind's benevolent, God-directed future spills from the pages like the momentous visions she has been given. It takes great courage to share these experiences with the public who too often are quick to ridicule and even worse, dismiss. I commend Claire for the work she has done, for writing a book is a daunting task. Even more, I honor her for never closing herself off to the divine and for allowing Mother Mary, Jesus and the angels to visit her and use her as their vessel. "Let the person who has ears to hear, listen." Mark 4:9.

Catherine Lanigan, author of
Romancing the Stone,
Angel Tales, and *Divine Nudges*

Introduction

Each of us has a story to share, with experiences that have guided our lives in ways that profoundly move us, teach us, heal us, and ultimately awaken us. It has been said that sharing personal stories is one of the most effective ways to offer inspiration for the hearts and minds of those who wish to receive. My stories are shared from a deep place in my heart, and are reflections that may be recognized as the Divine that is within us all. Whether we have recognized them or not, we each have experienced reflections of the Divine on our journey in unique and powerful ways. We sing them, write them, speak them, dance them, paint them, create and live them.

When I asked Mother Mary why she requested that I write this book, she answered "for Spiritual nourishment." There is so much more to who we all are than what we sometimes allow ourselves to be aware of. I recognize that part of the leap that humanity is in the process of is waking up to just how miraculous these times are, and how capable we are of pulling out all the stops and rising to our fullest potentials. Something, indeed, is happening that we can already feel.

Change is part of a beginning, and humanity is in the midst of great change. We are witnessing the importance of making new choices for a more sustainable future, using our awakened hearts, compassion, creative expression, and cooperative Spirit. Amidst the shifts occurring are rising planetary changes, concerns of nuclear radiation, wars, heightened solar activity, etc. We all want to stay close to the vision that, through all of this, we are evolving and on the verge of a new consciousness that is rising as well. That consciousness supports a global family authentically living together in peace and unity; not only for the people of our planet, but all life-forms, and our beloved planet herself.

Saint Augustine offered great wisdom when he said; "Miracles are not contrary to nature, but only contrary to what we know about nature." The things that we do not understand we call miracles; and things happen all the time that we do not have a conventional explanation for. No matter what we call these things, there is an undeniable knowing that they come from a loving source beyond what we might imagine in our everyday lives.

As we move through this time of transition and transformation we will reach deeper within ourselves for greater understanding and further into our creative gifts to support the incredible change that we are up for. Marianne Williamson poignantly shares *"Faith isn't blind; it's visionary. It enables us to see beyond what's happening, to what could be happening."*

There have been numerous occasions when I faced a seeming challenge that was just as much a journey in faith as the next person. I was left poised to use my gifts and abilities to create a solution, which in some ways, helped speed up my own evolutionary process. I always knew there were heavenly presences by my side offering their loving energy, and for whatever reason I was going through such a challenge I would find out when the time came for me to know. Through our resilience we move past whatever apprehension there might be about our future, and remember that the powerful force of Love is enough to move mountains.

"It is not the events in our lives that create joy or misery. It is the meaning that we give those events. Whatever happens in your life, give it meaning that empowers you." – Denise Linn

I have changed some of the names in the stories to honor their privacy. I know for myself that many of the stories I have heard from others, and many of my own personal learning experiences have helped to light the way through some of the most challenging parts of my life, even today. Perhaps the sharing of these stories will offer a sense of hope and encouragement, and support an awareness that there is a world, and a part of ourselves, that exists beyond the physical life we see before us. The visitations from Mother Mary always exemplified that for me. All that I might have forgotten about the world that lay beyond this physical plane seems to fade into an expanded connection through her messages of love, opening my heart from the deepest part of my soul.

We came here on purpose with a purpose. Our true selves emerge as we walk the path we came to live. There is strength in knowing that there is a Divine plan at work, no matter what form things may appear to take along the way. Each of the stories shared in this book bring forth an offering that we are not alone, and we are greatly loved. Allow whatever speaks to your heart to blossom into a fuller expression of who you are and thrive in a way that is aligned with your soul's deepest calling.

Thank you for being a part of my journey.

Chapter One

A Gift, a Blessing and a Prayer

Peace will stand. It will carry forth in humanity's efforts to aid the planet and help humanity. We must all remember that we are all One family under God who can choose to participate in the betterment of mankind and the quality of life. ~ **Mother Mary, Mother of Jesus**

Life is filled with loving mystery and divine exploration. Our hearts are filled with awe of the miraculous, and longing for a greater understanding of what the meaning of life in the Universe is all about. We seek answers in many places, journey to distant lands for clues, and gaze at the heavens for signs. Then something awakens a knowing within, one that is beyond what you thought you ever knew, revealing a new road to travel. You glance back for a moment to see where you thought you were going, only to see that the path always led to where you are now. You are not pushed to move forward in this seeming new direction, yet are called with every fiber of your being to take flight on the beckoning journey that lies ahead. And fly you must, for you know it is part of who you are, and how you came into being. She speaks without a sound, and carries love across the ages, listen with your heart and you shall know what you have come to know, and awaken to what is already within.

* * *

As a child, I had many experiences that some would call different from the normal life. They ranged from out of body experiences, premonitions, prophetic dreams, and sensing non physical presences in the room, to seeing beautiful colors of light around people, which I later learned were called auras. I was quite comfortable with seeing auras, and I still see them to this day. I always had a natural sense of wonder about and love for God, yet I had no religious upbringing to speak of. My family did not go to church; however, on occasion I spent a Saturday night with a friend, and I would accompany them to church the next day.

The extra sensory gifts were not extra at all to me, but a natural part of who we are. Somehow I knew that others had these "gifts" as well, and was unsure why they did not give their gifts much attention. It was the unknown, an area of life seldom talked about among people I grew up around. I did not know what to do with these things when they happened, most of the time they showed up seemingly from out-of-the-blue. When I would speak of these things to my family, except for a few occasions, there was little response. Most of the time they would politely shrug it off and go on about their business.

As I grew older I found ways to distract myself from the world of the unexplained and imitate the shrugging my family had taught me, as if it were the solution to make life appear more normal. I got quite good at it for many years. However, nothing could have prepared me for what was to come in 1989.

I was returning to my home in Houston from Los Angeles where I had spent three months working on pilot season and working as a guest host for my friend Carole Dean's TV show "Healthstyles." The plan was to return home, regroup, prepare for a new home in L.A., and begin my permanent position on the show. All that changed when I began to experience a new kind of awareness that is not easy to describe. While traveling back home by car, this new awareness was a spontaneous linking up to the Earth's spirit, which completely caught me by surprise.

While I gazed out the window enjoying some of the beautiful desert scenery along the way, something started to feel different. I began to feel a shift from not only seeing the Earth's physical beauty, but also feeling her intelligence and sentience. I suddenly became aware that Earth had a life and soul of her own intelligence, if you will. I could feel that she was a true being that was expressing her love back to me. I had not even realized that in the observation of her beauty, I was also feeling great love for her. I could feel her consciousness, her love for us (humanity) and the love that she is. She was communicating that she wanted us to know her love for us. Almost like the longing of a mother about to give birth using the touch of her hand upon her belly to communicate an incredible unconditional love for the child about to be born while waiting for her spoken words to finally be heard by the human ears of her child.

Every part of the mother's body vibrates with love; it is a constant flow. Even though audible words were not coming forth, it was radiating an energy I could feel, see, and receive; the inaudible communication she was sending was reaching me. This awareness did not seem to be new information; it seemed to be old information, ancient in fact, already within me, rising up from deep within to my conscious awareness, like a memory surfacing. It was as if my spirit had already known this truth about the Earth and was finally remembering. I could feel her thoughts, her feelings, her past, and something about what her purpose of being was.

An overwhelming surge of emotions came over me that brought me to tears. This life changing awareness and experience made the days ahead challenging. I could not think of much else for several weeks. I did not know how to communicate such a powerful revelation to anyone, nor did I know what to do with it. This was not something I had ever heard, or read about, before. There would be no distraction or shrugging that would tear me away from the astonishing heart opening experience I had with the Earth that day.

A couple of weeks later, I saw a TV newscast showing footage of dolphins getting caught in tuna nets. The report showed fishermen pulling nets from the ocean filled with live tuna and dolphins that were being poured onto the deck of a ship. They were gathering up the tuna; however, the dolphins were left on the deck without concern for returning them to their home in the ocean. The fishermen seemed to have no emotion; as if they had done their work that way for so long that it had become second nature. It seemed they were oblivious to the senseless waste of life of an innocent species. The goal was the tuna and the money that the tuna represented, and nothing else mattered.

I fell to my knees in shock while witnessing this despairing newscast. I shuddered at the thought of what would happen with our world if the lack of consciousness displayed by the fishermen was simply a microcosm of the larger picture at hand.

"My God, how could we be doing this to ourselves?" I thought. Those nets represented greed, and the dolphins were not only the innocent lives of their own species, but also represented the innocent lives of all beings; yours, mine, Earth, her environment, and every creature here on Earth. We had been getting caught in our own nets of greed and forgetfulness of who we all really are, who we are as One with all life. The new awareness of our Earth as a living being had brought me a deeper awareness about All life on this planet. I prayed for the first time in a long time. Through my tears, I asked God to let me help; to show me how I could help inspire others to reawaken to what we are doing, and make more conscious choices; to remember that we are all connected.

After weeks of gathering all the books and information I could find on how to take better care of our planet and get recycling started in my neighborhood, I began my journey of sharing this new found knowledge with as many people as I could get to listen. Wonderful strides were made; a few neighborhood leaders joined together with me and recycling pickup became a new addition to our community. One by one, I visited grocery stores and restaurants asking them to use only dolphin safe tuna; and paper, or plastic cups, instead of Styrofoam. It was now 1990, and manufacturers had not yet abolished the CFCs found in Styrofoam.

My passion for educating as many people and businesses as possible about eco-friendly living kept me very busy. Then, a few months later, something interesting happened. I started to have, what felt like, inner messages that I could feel, see, and hear altogether as an inner communication. A lot like the experience I had with the Earth in her communion with me. This inner voice said, "Claire, this is all good (referring to the work I was doing to help Earth), and there is something more." "What more good could there be than helping the planet?" I thought. I was soon to find out what that "more" would be, little bit by little bit.

A few days later the inner voice brought another message, "Something really big is going to happen with the planet; you're going to help (in some way). Your gifts are going to increase and will be used to help."

Somehow I knew this message heralded profound changes for the Earth and humanity. Once again, I felt that I was being reminded of something I already knew in my heart, and it was time to start remembering it. I later learned that there have been visionaries, and the like, who have spoken of great changes for humanity and Earth, however I had no exposure to this information at that time.

For days I stammered around trying to understand these inner "Western Union" messages. Questions like - what is this really big thing that is going to happen with the planet, where were these messages coming from, how am I supposed to help? ... all occupied my mind. I could no longer look at life in the same way. The focus that I used to put on my career would now be devoted to understanding what these messages were all about. My heart longed to be more of service in whatever I could do to help.

My dreams became more vivid and intense. I would dream events at night and then see them happen on the news the next day, or see them up to two weeks out. Sometimes, in the middle of the day, I would see a future event as a vision or during a meditation. The things I was being shown would usually be an environmental event that was about to take place in a very specific area, like a huge mudslide in San Francisco or a massive outbreak of tornadoes in Houston. I saw the Northridge earthquake in LA three days before it happened. My heart would go out to the people in these areas as I prayed for them to be protected from harm.

One night I was awoken by a presence in the room. It was a brilliant white light with thin streams of rainbow/ opalescence colors bursting outward. The tremendous love that emanated from this light was so immense I wanted to bask within the experience for the rest of my life. There was a feminine energy about this light that felt familiar to me. My heart was excited beyond belief. A thought flashed through my mind "It's finally happening!" But I did not consciously know what "it" was that was finally happening. I just knew it was something I had waited for all my life.

Mary's Lullaby – a Gift, a Blessing, and a Prayer

A couple of months later, while curled up one evening on my living room couch reading, I noticed it was getting late and decided to retire to bed. As I got up to close the blinds I was stopped by an intense feeling heralding an incredible presence in the room. I could feel a shift in energy that brought a tingling sensation; swirling light began to encircle me and a beautiful song began pouring from my lips, it was so beautiful that I was swept away in its powerful peace and love. It was a song that I had never heard before. A message followed, heard both in the room and as an inner voice saying "This song is a gift, a blessing, and a prayer."

At the same time, like a Technicolor TV screen, a vision flashed before me, and I saw people singing this song in their homes, from many places, and many walks of life. I saw them all at once, as if it were through the eyes of God. They were surrounded in the same kind of light that was encompassing me, and I could see past them, through their windows. Huge storms of great magnitude were raging outside, the strongest winds I had ever seen, however, the people were in total peace inside...as if they had no concern about the massive storms. Their faith was strong; there was a joy about them, and love was beaming from their faces.

The message continued..."This song will be sung in many homes." I somehow knew the song would be recorded, and that the right people, place and time would come together for this to happen. Moments later the vision was gone, and I was left standing there in blissful gratitude. "Oh my God," I spoke out loud. What I had seen, heard, and felt was beyond words.

As soon as I could gather my composure, I grabbed my tape recorder and quickly sang the song so that I would not forget the words and melody. I had never written a song before; and this came from a whole different source beyond me. A heavenly presence had entered my living room that night, swirled around and through me, brought the nectar of love through the song from my lips, and flashed a vision of the future before my eyes. A gift had just been given, one that was not only for me, but for others who would also benefit from the reminder this song brings...a reminder that the peace and love we seek is already within.

A couple of days later my dear friend Cheryl and her husband came to town for a visit. I will mention that Cheryl's husband is a famous song writer, but for his privacy, I will not mention his name. While we were getting caught up on news about our families the thought crossed my mind to share the song that Mother Mary brought. I was not quite ready to talk about the experience that came along with it yet, but I did want to share the song. I kept it simple and casually asked if they would like to hear a song that recently came to me. I could see their delight as they enthusiastically said yes. I began to sing while they sweetly smiled. Then Cheryl's husband spoke up and said "Claire, that song is beautiful, it's a lullaby." "A lullaby" I said, "you know it's good to know what type of song this is." I just don't know why yet as I chuckled to myself.

A few days later it was time for the next prayer meditation gathering with a group of friends, we had been meeting once a week for a couple of months by this time. I arrived just in time for the meeting to start. We began with prayer, moving into meditation and settling into a peaceful state. In that moment one of the ladies began to speak, she said that Mother Mary was present in the room with us, "She has a message, there is a song, and it's a lullaby, would that person please sing it."

My heart began to race. I thought to myself "I haven't mentioned this song yet to them, there's no way they could possibly have known this ahead of time." At that moment I could feel the same light energy build around me that I had experienced the night the song and vision first came. As I began singing, it felt like a strong pulsing heartbeat from the center of the universe came into my own chest, and then, in a single motion, the room was filled with blissful song and prayer. A bright light began swirling in and around me. I was once again in a space of deep peace and love, much like the first night the song came.

When the song was over, I braced myself for what was to come next. My friend's faces were all lit up, and glowing with smiles, each expressing a similar feeling of the experience. They told me that I should record the song; that it was so beautiful and peaceful that it should be out there for more people. I shared with them what had happened the night the song first came, and that I was left with a feeling that somehow the song was going to be recorded, I just didn't know how, or when. We all stood in humble amazement of what had just taken place, a visitation from Mother Mary, and the beautiful gift of love she had brought to us. I would soon see everything I had been told come to pass.

The following week, a friend, CJ, called from Los Angeles to recommend that I read the book "Mary's Message to the World" by Annie Kirkwood. She didn't know that I had just purchased the book after one of my friends had told me about it from the meditation meeting. CJ knew someone who knows the author, and for some reason, wanted me to have the phone number that had been given to her. "Annie lives in Dallas" she said, "you travel there all the time don't you, maybe you should meet her." Now, this was getting more interesting by the day, "How did she even know to call me about this subject out of the blue?" I thought. In my amazement I thankfully took the number. After we hung up, I sat there quietly for a moment to ponder why this message was passed along to me to call Annie. Nothing really came; it just seemed to be the right thing to do. I curiously dialed the number, no one answered, so I put the number aside.

Before I knew it, about a week later, I was on my way to Dallas for some business.

Jim, a close friend of mine, invited me to stay at his home while I was there, which was in the heart of Dallas. I would only be in town a couple of days, but brought the book "Mary's Message to the World" with me in case I would have some time to read. I only had a few chapters left to go. While having dinner, Jim shared about his wonderful job at the radio station where he produced a talk show. I was very happy for him; he seemed to really love producing. Jim had been working in radio for a while and recently moved from Houston to Dallas, he was picking up his new life there beautifully.

It was a long day and I decided to retire early, but not without doing a little reading before I went to sleep. When I pulled my copy of "Mary's Message to the World" out of the suite case I had a strong feeling that I would be showing the book to Jim. He was still in the dining room finishing up a cup of tea when I entered the room. "Jim, I'd like to show you this amazing book that I am reading." I laid the book on the table before him. He was astounded at the timing and said "I just had that author on the radio talk show that I produce last week; I have her number, would you like it?" I stood in shared amazement...I now had a second friend offer Annie's number, friend's who didn't even know each other...and within a week's time span. It felt like I had just gotten another "universal tap on the shoulder" to try to reach her again. But it will have to wait until morning.

The morning was full of anticipation over what seemed to be something of great importance around my contacting Annie. Hopefully I would have the chance to solve this mystery before I would leave for my business meeting. Her number was still lying by the phone where I left it; I took a deep breath and began to dial. A sweet voice answered right away with a warm hello. Relieved that I was able to reach her, I briefly shared that I had been reading her book and let her know how much it meant to me to connect with her. She was very kind in her reply, "thank you, Mary's messages have meant a lot to me as well." I explained, "People keep giving me your number, do you have any idea why this is happening?" Annie said that there was going to be a gathering the following week where an apparition of Mother Mary was expected to occur "maybe that is why you were suppose to contact me, so that you can join us" she said.

It took a bit of work, but everything that I needed to get there fell into place miraculously. When that day arrived, about fifty people gathered expectantly on a clear, sunny day at Joe Pool Lake, just outside Dallas. After a brief prayer and meditation, we saw the sun begin to spin, then split into two swirling suns. The children who were present called out in their excitement that they could see Mother Mary appearing before them, while we all experienced a great wave of peace blanketing the area.

I saw breathtaking waves of rainbow colors spinning out from the sun. All I could do was stand in awe of the presence of miracles taking place before us. It was as if God wanted us there to receive a more solid knowing of the presence of Love that is continually and eternally here for us. Whether we see it and feel it, or not, it is always here. As I returned home to Houston, all the way home I thanked God for the Love, and for the opportunity to be present for such a powerful confirmation of the miracles in our lives.

A month later I received a phone call from the author's husband, Byron. He asked if I would be interested in being the voice of Mother Mary for the book on tape "Mary's Message to the World." It was such an honor to be asked to share, and a blessing to be of service. The connection I felt with Mother Mary, by this time, had changed my life. Over the weeks, Mother Mary had been bringing messages to me in dreams, meditations, and sometimes while taking walks. They ranged from locutions, which is like a telepathic communication, to luminous visions that would appear in the room. There was even a time when she appeared in a church accompanied by two angels in all her radiant traditional beauty. I could see an arching rainbow of light, almost like a huge bubble around her, and could also see the angels who accompanied her. There were many people there that night; quite a few of them took photographs while the visitation was in progress. I later discovered that the vision I had seen of Mother Mary that night, with the rainbow bubble of light, had shown up in one of the photographs as well.

It was an honor to be asked to serve by being a voice for Mother Mary and help in sharing her messages. When I asked Byron how he knew that I did professional voice-over work "We didn't know that," was his reply. When Annie came to the phone, she said "Mary chose you Claire, just like she chose me." She continued "When I asked Mary who was to be her voice, she answered "ask Claire." I accepted in humble gratitude to be a part of sharing the messages from the book.

On the third day, while recording the unabridged version of "Mary's Message to the World," after several hours of reading, my eyes began to tire and it was time for a short break. While sipping water and resting my eyes, I began to feel the strong presence of Mother Mary. She comes with a powerful sense of love that moves through me and around the room, much like a window that opens up, bringing a fresh breath of air, filled with the softness of rose petals and the warmth of a mother's loving arms. The words, "It is time to sing the song now" moved through me as a locution. The message lightly tapped me on the shoulder, like a gentle reminder of something already destined to begin its sojourn.

I confided to the producer who was still sitting in the engineering room that I had a beautiful song from Mother Mary, and asked him if he would like to hear it. He said yes as he loaded a dat tape. Just as I began to take in a deep breath to begin singing, I could feel, and begin to see, more presences in the room. Now, joined by Mother Mary were Jesus, angels, and other heavenly beings. They filled the room with a luminous glow, the walls disappeared, and the light seemed to go on for eternity.

A tingling sensation began to build around me as I felt a resonance quickening in every cell of my body. Loving energy filled the room. I felt everything merge within me. As I began to sing, bliss filled my whole being. They were vibrating their love through the sound of my voice. Once the last word was sung, I could no longer see the presences, but I could still feel the echo of the blissful state of heaven that had just merged with this world. I sat in quiet reverence of what had just taken place. As I slowly peered through the window of the engineering room, I could see the producer and engineer gazing into the room, speechless. Although they couldn't see the apparitions, I could tell by their faces that they knew something profound had just happened. That day, the prophecy Mother Mary had given a month earlier - that the song would be recorded - was fulfilled.

They asked permission to add Mary's Lullaby to the audio book of "Mary's Message to the World" as a theme song, I whole heartedly agreed. As word got out about Mary's Lullaby there were many people who wanted to have a copy of the tape. It was clear that it was time to also release Mary's Lullaby as a separate musical tape for those who wanted to play it regularly in their homes. The word about the tape had far reaching effects. I received phone calls and letters from people who shared their warm hearted stories of the experiences they were having from hearing the song. There were also meditation groups in the U.S., Canada, Mexico, Europe, and Australia that contacted me to share that they were playing Mary's Lullaby as a regular part of their practice at their meetings. The song is now available to listen to on my website at LightedPaths.org. As Mother Mary had said when she first brought the song, "this song will be sung in many homes," her prophecy had become a reality.

There is one more event that I'm compelled to share - one that speaks to the miracles of the human Spirit. After the recording of Mary's Lullaby, in the Spring of 1994, I was traveling in the Texas hill country with a friend. We stopped off in a little town called Marble Falls to talk with some realtors. Just as we arrived, phone calls started coming in to their office about a huge storm headed their way with incredibly strong winds, large hail and intense lightening. It was a strange thing; I recalled that the sky was very cloudy; some of the clouds were mildly dark, but it did not look like the large storm being described by the calls that were coming in.

The receptionist announced that she had just received a fifth call about the storm and nervously began heading for the door. "I'm going to move my car to shelter" she said. As she passed by me I shared with her, "Do you know that you can be in the middle of a raging storm and still be protected?" She had just reached the door and turned around "No, I didn't know that, how is it done?" she asked. "Through prayer," I replied. She smiled in relief, thanked me for the reminder, and said she would be back in a few minutes.

Moments later the storm struck the little town. The electricity went out in the tiny mobile trailer office, as the building began to rock. Standing in the dark, looking out the window, we witnessed at least 60 mile an hour winds or greater. No one in the room had ever experienced a storm that fierce in their town. Fear was escalating among the staff, one of the ladies began to cry, and I felt deeply compelled to try to calm the situation as much as I could. "It's OK, everything will be OK," I reassured them. They continued to lose confidence in their safety, so I spoke again, "We can stand here looking out the window, talking about how scary it is, or we can do something about it." "What's that?" said someone with a shaken voice. I replied, "We can pray."

They each commented that it was a good idea, but were quickly distracted again by the heightening activity outside the window. Flying debris began crashing against the large window where we were standing in the reception area of the office. As we peered out the window, we could see the tall bush outside that proudly stood high when we first arrived become completely flattened by the pelting rain and wind. The rain was so thick that we couldn't see past the bush; it was only about a foot from the building we were in. I cannot say how I knew, because I could not actually see one, but I knew that there was a tornado out there on the ground and headed our way.

At that moment, I began experiencing the strong inner voice of Mother Mary saying, "Claire sing, and sing now." "Mother Mary, how am I going to do this when they are so frightened that I cannot hold their attention?" I asked. She answered with the same words "Sing, and sing now." So, I took a deep breath, and asked the others, "Would you like to hear a song?" To my utter amazement, they broke their fear-filled trance and unanimously replied, "Yes."

"Quickly, gather some chairs and have a seat" I said. As they formed a semi-circle around me I noticed that my hands were slightly shaking, and at the same time, I felt solidly calm within. I sat down on the couch directly behind me, which was right in front of the big window. Not a wise choice you might say? I couldn't agree with you more … with a tornado outside, who knows how close, a window would be the last place one would want to sit near. However, that was where I felt I was to sit – possibly to demonstrate faith. Who knows? But sit there I did.

I took one more deep breath and Mary's Lullaby began pouring forth. A soothing balm of peace seemed to lift the fear from the room as each person began to settle into a calm space. Their faces changed; they looked almost child like – there was a beautiful innocence about them as if something within them had shifted to a more angelic-like state. The woman who had been crying earlier reached out and took the hand of the man sitting next to her. Each of them lovingly glanced at each other as if to say, "We made it through the storm."

I could tell that the sound of the storm that was massively surging moments before had come to a complete calm. I turned around to look out the window in hopes that I was hearing correctly…what I witnessed was what seemed no less than a miracle. Just as suddenly and swiftly as the storm had landed on us, it left in the same way. As I sat in awe staring out the window my heart was filled with wondrous gratitude. Then I heard one of the ladies say "That song was so peaceful...where did it come from?" I turned around, and through tears of joy I replied "I guess you could say it came from heaven." It was then that I realized that another one of the earlier visions Mother Mary brought had manifested that day - the song was inspiring inner peace as storms raged outside.

We all stepped outside and could see where the tornado had just struck a huge tree directly across the street. It had been completely uprooted. The whole town experienced tremendous destruction; it looked as though bombs had been dropped throughout the town. National news reported the devastation, by that evening President Bill Clinton declared the area a national disaster.

Below is just one of many articles that had been written about the storm:

Atmospheric Archive: May 13th

By Steve LaNore, Dallas Weather Examiner

May 13, 1994 Marble Falls, TX: F-3 (158-206mph) tornado

The tornado entered the city from the west. It crossed a densely-developed business and residential area. Roofs were severely damaged and several buildings were partially destroyed. Boats at a dealership (Lake LBJ is nearby) were tossed on top of each other.

Two-by-four's were driven into the side of a church preschool care center, penetrating inside to a classroom some four to five feet. The blessing: all children had been moved into the hallways just moments before the tornado got there. Signs were blown down with hundreds of buildings suffering roof damage.

Marble Falls primary school was hit, but students had been evacuated to the main school. Metal I-beams bent at a nearby metal building indicated damage consistent with 150 mph winds. The local Walmart was hit and severely damaged, with the employees (who had taken cover) sustaining only a few minor injuries.

Marble Falls High School also sustained damage from the tornado. Students had just finished a weather drill as the storm struck.

In all, over 440 homes sustained damage, with one house and 17 mobile homes destroyed, and major damage to 36 homes. Eighteen businesses reported major damage with 47 others reporting minor damage. In addition, two bridges were damaged, along with severe damage to schools. In all, 512 structures sustained damage.

The path ranged to half a mile wide and it was four miles long, although it may have skipped along for several miles before entering the city. There were about a dozen other tornadoes in Texas this same day, but none of the size or strength of this one.

Total losses in the tens of millions; amazingly only one injury.

Examiner.com Atmospheric Archive: May 13th - Dallas Weather | Examiner.comhttp://www.examiner.com/weather-in-dallas/atmospheric-archive-may-13th#ixzz1feA5EOUG

* * *

I have seen the awesome transformation that can occur when we open our awareness to the miracles that happen daily. Our hearts reawaken, and our true spirit of limitlessness comes forth, no matter the circumstances in life.

Mother Mary has shared this message... "Peace will stand. It will carry forth in humanity's efforts to aid the planet and help humanity. We must all remember that we are all One Family under God, and members of the human race who can choose to participate in the betterment of mankind and the quality of life." May it be in Love.

Chapter Two

Connecting Beyond Time and Space

To believe in something not yet proved and to underwrite it with our lives: it is the only way we can leave the future open. ~ **Lillian Smith**

Most of my adult life I have had a strong interest in technologies and systems that better support the health of our planet and humanity. When I heard about the New Sciences Conference in Fort Collins, Colorado, I was happy to see that their exploration in this topic was vast. I walked into the sun room where my friend Sandy had just finished meditating on her morning guidance. I shared with her about the conference, knowing it would be up her alley too. She said she had gotten a message of "It's time to go" that morning, and that was what she was meditating on. She looked at the flier and said the energy of "It's time to go" was all over it. We both felt that we were meant to be there and decided to make the journey together. I contacted a friend of mine, Diana, who lives in Fort Collins, to see if there might be a chance that I could visit with her sometime during our trip, we had not seen each other in a long time. As it turned out, she was scheduled to speak at the conference about her work and research on intentional communities.

This was icing on the cake to not only see Diana, but to hear her speak on this very important topic. Her home was not too far from the conference hotel where we were planning to stay, so she asked if we would like to stay in one of her spare rooms at her home instead. I could not have asked for a better chance to spend some time with her. Sandy agreed, so we accepted her invitation. A few days later we were all packed and ready to make the 1100 mile journey from Houston to Fort Collins.

There was quite a turnout the first day of the conference. People came from all over the world to attend. The hotel where the conference was being held was packed, and all the rooms were booked up. Inventors, experts on renewable energy, researchers in healing technologies, and the like, were presenting their wisdom on new sciences that were not yet common knowledge in the mainstream. There were also related topics that would pique the interest of seekers in spirituality, higher consciousness, and extraterrestrial studies.

The day was filled with a plethora of intriguing speakers. I took a lot of notes and met so many wonderful people. By dinnertime Sandy and I joined a few conference goers that we met throughout the day for a bite to eat in the hotel café. Sandy and I spent a few minutes going over the rest of the itinerary together, noting the things we wanted to do the rest of the evening. Cell phones had not become popular yet, neither of us had one, so we relied on good planning to get us by. I was interested in hearing Dr. Steven Greer (DisclosureProject.org) speak about his research in extraterrestrial studies, and Sandy wanted to stay in the cafe and visit with her new friends, David and Barbara, from New Zealand. The timing seemed to lay out perfectly for us both to accomplish our goals and then meet up after the presentation. We decided the best place to connect again would be in the meeting room where Greer's talk was being held. A couple of other new friends at the dinner table, Roberta and Mark, said they would join me for Dr. Greer's presentation. We set off early to get signed in knowing that this popular event would likely be standing room only.

It was a fascinating talk to say the least. Greer shared stories of how he and his team had been conducting scientific research and field experiments to help further humanity's understanding of extraterrestrial intelligences. I could have hung around for days to hear more of his amazing accounts and adventures.

It was nearing the end of Dr. Greer's talk when he invited the audience to participate in a guided meditation led by him. He directed us to get comfortable in our seats, close our eyes, and inhale deep relaxing breaths. Through our imaginations, we were taken on a visual exploration where we were greeted by a guide who invited us to go on a spiritual journey. The meditation was deeply moving, it was a joy to join so many people whose hearts were open to the experience. After the meditation, we were asked to pick a partner and share our thoughts. Roberta and I were sitting right next to each other so we turned our chairs, face to face, and took turns talking about what the experience was like for us.

Greer's presentation ran about 10 minutes over the allotted time, but no one seemed to mind. He was cheered on with a standing ovation by a very delighted audience. As late nights go, the room began to empty while Roberta and I waited for Sandy to meet up with us. Ten minutes turned into twenty, then forty. By now, it was just Roberta and me left in the room talking. Finally, I decided to stick my head out the door to take a glance around the corridor. No Sandy in sight. We waited a few minutes longer and then decided to take a look around the rest of the meeting rooms just in case she went to the wrong one. They were all vacant, Dr. Greer's talk was the only presentation scheduled for the evening. We were both perplexed as to what might have happened.

The next step was to go take a look around the little café where we had dinner to see if she might still be visiting with her friends David and Barbara. On our way, we ran into David in the hallway, he said that Sandy had left on time to meet us in the presentation room where Dr. Greer had been speaking. My sense was that Sandy must have missed us somehow and thought I had gotten a ride to Diana's house. It was quite late by this time; too late to call my friend Diana to see if Sandy had arrived. Diana would be giving her talk first thing in the morning; I did not want to disturb her sleep when she would need a good night's rest. Roberta and David were interested in a cup of coffee at the café which gave us a chance to put our heads together on what to do next.

One thing I can say about Sandy, she is very dependable and would never intentionally change a plan without a very good reason for it. I somehow knew that where ever she might be, she was all right; I did not sense any danger around her. It was now 12:45 AM. Roberta offered to take me to Diana's house in hopes that Sandy might already be there. I shared the location and started to grab my things. After looking at her watch, Roberta said "Well, I guess that idea is out. The gas stations around here close at midnight and my tank is too low to get you to Diana's home and back without a fill up."

The hotel was completely booked; getting a room would be out of the question. Roberta said she already had a room at the hotel. She did not want to make the long trek to Denver where she lived and then make it back to Fort Collins early in the morning. "You're welcome to stay with me in my room tonight" offered Roberta. Gratefully I accepted, and was glad I had a spare toothbrush in my purse.

The room had two very comfy looking double beds; a welcome sight after a long day of events. Before retiring I headed off to the bathroom to wash up. It was now 1:15 AM; I was feeling a bit concerned about not being able to get in touch with Sandy to let her know I was okay.

I have always known that people are far more connected than we might think. This connection is beyond time and space. Communication can be sent through feeling and thought in ways that are limitless. Knowing how sensitive Sandy is, I thought that if I were to connect heart to heart with her, she might be able to, at least, have a sense that everything was all right. While standing in front of the mirror I closed my eyes, centered myself in my heart and visualized Sandy. I then spoke these words out loud, "Sandy, I'm okay. I'm staying at the hotel with Roberta and will call you first thing in the morning. There's no need to worry about me."

When I awoke the next morning at 7:30 AM, I immediately picked up the phone and called Diana's house. Sandy picked up the phone right away "Hello? Claire?" Relieved, I said "Good morning Sandy, I'm so happy to hear your voice." With equal enthusiasm Sandy replied "Same here! At 1:15 AM, I woke up and saw you standing in the room talking to me. I saw Mother Mary standing on one side of you, and Jesus standing on the other side." Intrigued, I asked Sandy what I said. "You said that you were okay, that you were staying at the hotel with Roberta, and you would call me first thing in the morning. Claire, it was no dream, I was wide awake. And that's why I knew it was you when I answered the phone" she said. It was the exact time that I had sent the message to her. She also did not have foreknowledge of Roberta having a room at the hotel.

"It worked Sandy; I really did send that exact message to you." I shared how I connected with her heart to heart and worked to send the message. "Thank you for being so receptive Sandy." We both expressed how relieved we were that both of us were okay. I told Sandy about the events of last night's puzzling evening and asked what happened. With surprise she said "You were not in the room where Greer had been speaking. I looked there, and all over for you. I caught the lady at the check-in table just before she was leaving and asked if I was at the right place for Dr. Greer's talk … she pointed to the room that you said you'd be in. When I opened the door, there was no one in there. I turned around to tell the woman the room was empty but she was already gone. It was right at 10 PM, the time you said the event would be over."

I remembered that Greer's talk went about 10 minutes over, but how could she have missed us. "Right at the time you would have shown up, we were all completing a guided meditation, but you saw no one in the room?" I asked. "The room was empty except for the chairs and podium. So I looked around the immediate area to see if you might be close by. When I didn't find you, I figured we must have missed each other somehow and you might have gotten a ride back to Diana's, and I was being guided to go home and get to bed." she replied.

We both paused for a moment and took in all that had been said. Sandy needed to get on the road to make it in time for the first speaker, so we decided to talk more over tea at the next break. Steven Greer had said he was taking us on a journey. Could that journey have made us invisible to this dimension? It was a mystery we may not ever truly solve, however we both were grateful for having a greater understanding of the unseen gifts that we all possess. We had the opportunity to connect telepathically with each other through our hearts, and could see how real and viable an option it is.

Some people would call it bi-location because Sandy actually saw me standing in the room while communicating with her. Having heavenly escorts join you when you are in need of sending a message makes it all the sweeter. This type of communication is available to everyone, and I now use it whenever I need to connect and have no physical way of doing it. I encourage anyone to begin exploring what is possible when hearts open and connect with other hearts. It's a beautiful and magical experience.

Chapter Three

The Path of Miracles

A few years ago I had a dream that showed me how miraculous life can be when followed with the heart.

In the dream, I was driving down the freeways of Los Angeles on a beautiful sunny California day. I ended up at a small strip of a white sandy beach with crystal blue waters and about twenty or so people romping and having fun. They didn't seem to notice me standing there, almost as if I was invisible. I was dressed in business attire, a dark blue dress, stockings and dress shoes. I walked toward the shoreline, stopped, looked down at my right hand and in it was a Miraculous Medal.

The thought came to me that I needed to throw it into the ocean, but I didn't know if it would make it that far. I drew my hand back as far as I could, then gave a forward thrust with all my might and threw it into the water. All of a sudden an explosion of Light burst before me, and encompassed me. I didn't know exactly what was happening, but I knew it was something wonderful.

When I awoke I remember thinking, "Wow, what an Amazing dream, not sure what that was all about though." It had the feeling of a Divine origin, and left me with a strong sense of hope.

It was time to get dressed and head out to my new job anchoring traffic on Houston's news station KTRH. It was my first time to do live broadcast radio, and I was pretty nervous. I sprang out of bed, got dressed, and headed out the door.

My mother's house was on the way, and as it turned out, there was plenty of extra time so I decided to make a quick stop off at her place to say hello.

After our hugs, she mentioned that she had found something on the floor in a used book store and somehow knew that she was supposed to give it to me. As she placed it in my right hand, I looked down and saw that it was a Miraculous Medal.

"Mom, this is amazing, I just had a dream this morning where a Miraculous Medal showed up in my right hand."

"Really?"

"Yes. I think that's very interesting. But good interesting. Well, I gotta go. I'll tell you more about it later" I said.

She gave me a big kiss on the cheek and sent me off with a snack for later.

As I walked into the studio there was an older man with a kind looking face sitting in a wheel chair at a long white counter with a microphone in front of him delivering the latest traffic report on the air. A moment later he removed his headphones and smiled as he introduced himself.

"Hi I'm Steve, you must be Claire."

Before I could open my mouth a thought shot through my head, "So how long do you think you're going to be in that wheel chair?"

I gasped at such a confrontational thought, not being a very confrontational person, I couldn't imagine myself even thinking such a pointed question.

"Y…Yes, I'm Claire. Very nice to meet you," I finally got the words out.

And then the most extraordinary thing happened. He answered my unspoken question without having spoken it out loud as he pointed to his wheel chair saying "Ohhh, you mean this"?

"Oh my God," I thought to myself. He had actually heard my thought. I silently squirmed… "Uh…yes, that." (I gestured toward his chair).

Now you're probably asking yourself why would she just answer him as if she really asked the question out loud. Well, by this point in my journey, there have already been a number of unexplainable events I've been party to. I decided not to fight it and to go with the flow, curiously following the trail of where this was leading.

He quite matter of factly shared, "I've been in this chair almost six months now, my doctor says that my condition is only going to get worse because my legs have degenerated too much to ever recover and walk again. The tough part has been to learn to emotionally adjust to the situation."

My heart sank and went into full overdrive compassion for this sweet spirit of a man. Before I could stop myself, words began to pour from my mouth, "I don't believe that you have to be in that wheel chair the rest of your life. There's so much you can do for your health. There are all kinds of holistic methods out there to support you, and besides that ... I believe in miracles!"

Suddenly, I stopped, realizing my mouth had run away with my thought. In my head, I silently reprimanded myself. "Uhhhhhhh!!!! Claire, what are you doing? You don't have a right to get this man's hopes up about something like that."

He looked at me with a somewhat startled but grateful look on his face, almost like he came to a realization that he was in the presence of a close family member in whom he could confide.

I realized I had already gone past the point of no return in "coming out" with where I thought this conversation might be going at this point.

"Steve, may I share with you an example of a miracle"?

He nodded with intrigue.

"Let me tell you about a dream I had just last night."

I told him about the dream of the miraculous medal and how my mother had just handed me a miraculous medal on my way into the studio. Steve stayed glued to every word.

Then I asked "Do you know the story of the miraculous medal?"

"No, I don't" he replied.

"Well, I'm not Catholic, but I heard the story from a nun I recently met. The story goes like this. In the 1800's, I think it was around 1830, there was a young woman who was a nun of the Daughters of Charity in France. She was Catherine Laboure, and had an apparitional visit from Mother Mary, the mother of Jesus. Mary asked her to strike or have designed and formed, a medal of the vision that Catherine had been given of her. Then Catherine was to distribute the medals to the people because there was about to be a great challenge that would be coming soon. Mary said that the medals were a gift for the people and were to be thought of as a symbol of a prayer.

Shortly after that, Catherine convinced a priest to help her get the vision struck onto a medal and consequently, was able to get the medals out to the people of that area.

Within months, the bubonic plague hit Europe. Everyone who had received the medal did not perish from the plague.

Everyone who got the plague but later received a medal, also did not perish from the plague.

Thus the medal's name: Miraculous Medal."

Steve was staring at me dumbfounded but enthralled with the story.

"Steve, I think the idea that Mother Mary was trying to convey was that, with intention and prayer, there's always hope for a miracle."

He looked at me with tear-filled eyes while I pulled a miraculous medal out of my pocket. "It's so good to know that someone cares," he said.

"Steve, we all care. It's just that some of us have forgotten we care, and it gets covered up by the forgetfulness, but the care is still there," I replied.

Tears began to roll down his face. I reached for his hand and gently placed the medal into his palm, and silently said a very quick prayer for him.

We smiled at each other with an unspoken gratitude. The moment felt almost timeless.

It was almost time for my shift on the air to start, so we hugged and said our good byes.

I can remember taking my seat with my headphones in my hands about to go on the air, thinking how there really are no strangers in this world, and how close we all really are to one another. As I placed my headphones over my ears I could hear my producer letting me know I had fifteen seconds. I began to chuckle to myself as I noticed I wasn't as nervous as I thought I'd be.

Two days later I received a phone call from a friend of mine, Reverend Lucas. He mentioned that he had some business in Los Angeles relating to his work with the homeless and remembered that I used to live there. He thought I might be able to recommend a place for him to stay.

Reverend Lucas and I had spent a good amount of time together working with the homeless, from serving meals to offering healing services in his church. There were times when I would witness people moving beyond living on the streets, where Reverend Lucas was able to help them find steady employment and support them by having a place to stay.

As I shared some possible options for hotels in the area, Reverend Lucas asked if I might be able to go with him. He told me that my other two friends, Marylyn and Rhonda, were also going. He thought I might be able to be of some help.

As I explained that I had only just begun a new job and how I wasn't sure if I would be able to come up with the ticket money so soon, I remembered the dream I had only two days ago where I was in Los Angeles.

Then he said that Marylyn had an extra frequent flyer ticket that I could use.

There must be some reason that I need to go on this trip, I thought to myself.

How could I say no, it was too synchronistic to ignore?

"OK Reverend Lucas, just let me know the details and I'll be there."

I decided to take a Miraculous Medal with me, just in case I ended up at the ocean while we were there.

It was a beautiful sunny California day. We arrived at our hotel and were warmly greeted by a staff of helpers unloading our luggage into our rooms. Marylyn, Rhonda, and I were sharing a room together while Reverend Lucas had a room a few doors down. The first order of business was dinner, then off to work to go over our plans for the business meetings scheduled over the next couple of days.

I discovered that morning that we would be going to a meeting in Malibu at a restaurant called The Sand Castle. Even though Malibu is mostly cliffs and doesn't quite match the kind of beach I had in my dream I decided to take a Miraculous Medal with me anyway.

We were being seated when I looked out the window ahead and saw a small strip of a white sandy beach right outside the restaurant's back door. There were people romping and having fun in full beach attire and I could see beautiful crystal blue waves rise up from the ocean. As the waitress was handing us our menus, I asked how I might be able to slip outside to the beach for a moment.

She pointed to where the back door was and said "You know it's pretty strange, this is the first time I've ever seen this many people this time of year out there on the beach."

I pulled a Miraculous Medal out of my purse and excused myself, then headed straight for the back door.

As I stepped onto the sand I realized I was so caught up in the moment of the likeness of this beach and setting to my dream that I completely forgot that I was wearing high heeled shoes and stockings.

However, it didn't matter I told myself. I had come all this way and I was going for the ocean.

As I walked toward the shoreline, it didn't even seem to phase the onlookers that I was there, dressed in business attire.

I got as close to the water as I could and paused for a moment, watching the ebb and flow of the waves. "If I get any closer, the water will wash over my shoes and stocking feet. If I don't get close enough, I don't know if the medal will reach."

I drew my hand back as far as I could, then gave a forward thrust with all my might and threw it into the water. A giant wave reached up just at that moment and snatched the medal right in mid flight. I stood in awe at the timing and then began to notice my body vibrating, like electricity moving through me from head to toe. I knew something wonderful was happening, but I didn't know what.

When we got back to Houston and I returned to work, it happened to be on the same day that Steve was working the shift before me. He only worked on weekends because he had another job during the week. I made it to work just moments before my time to go on the air and quickly raced into the studio.

Steve had already kindly plugged my headphones in and waited for my entrance. I motioned a thankful wave as I hastily positioned myself for my first on air report. A couple moments later I was finished and I looked up at Steve to thank him, then noticed something different. There was no wheel chair.

There was no wheel chair!

Steve was standing up on his own two feet next to a cane that was leaning on the wall close by.

I looked at him in astonishment. "Steve, what happened"?

He said, "I just got mad at that chair and decided to get up and walk."

"Oh my God!" I said. "That's WONDERFUL. When did this happen?"

"Just a couple of days ago" he said.

I was in absolute awe of this incredible miracle that had taken place.

He looked at me very seriously. "Who are you? After meeting you my life has changed."

"Steve, I'm you," I said. "We are all the same. We are all one. It was YOU who decided to get up out of that chair and walk, with just a mustard seed of faith."

Spreading the Love

Mother Mary has come to modern day visionaries asking them to get the medals out to the people, throw them into oceans, rivers, lakes, ponds; put them under rocks, place them in school yards, etc. I have been doing this ever since I first heard about Mary's request.

The nun who first told me about the medals shared about the Association for the Miraculous Medal (http://www.amm.org/) in Perryville, Missouri. She said that I could easily order medals from them in large quantities, which I soon did.

I was very excited the day my first package of the medals arrived. As I walked in the door and sat down with my package, before I could even open it, Mother Mary made her presence known in the room. Her energy was very strong right from the start. She spoke to me in locution requesting that I open the package and place all the medals in my hands. I carefully opened the package and poured the tiny medals into my hands, all 100 of them. Once the last medal dropped into my hands from the package I eagerly waited for what was next. I could see a vision of Mary begin to appear before me as Our Lady of the Miraculous Medal. Her hands were slightly outstretched from her sides, just as she is traditionally depicted in the image on the medals. Then, there was light that began streaming from the palms of her hands all the way to the medals in my hands. There was a separate stream of light for every medal I was holding. As tears poured down my face, my heart sang for joy at the thought of everyone, and everyplace, that would receive these medals.

I have many stories that I could share about the journeys I have been on with these medals. Over the years I have had to replenish them many times due to the number of people and places I have shared them with.

A prayer always accompanies each medal when they are given to someone, along with a request for a blessing to be bestowed upon the land, water, and all who live and visit there.

On one occasion, while traveling home from the Rocky Mountain National Forest in Colorado, I had a most surprising event happen. We stopped off along side the road so that I could throw a medal into the Big Thompson River. As I stood in prayer, ready to toss the medal in, my friend pulled out his camera to take some shots. After the medal safely made its way into the water, I turned around and he quickly snapped a picture. When we later looked at the pictures, the one where I had just thrown a medal into the river had a large bright flash of light next to me. We couldn't explain how that got there when none of the pictures that had been taken in the same direction, just seconds apart, both before and after I threw a medal in the river, did not have the same flash of light. You can imagine our gratitude for having such a gift of what could possibly be Mary's presence showing up in one of the pictures. Perhaps she was letting us know all the more that she is lovingly present.

One more story that really stands out is when I was at one of my favorite little coffee places situated in a bookstore that sells both new and used books. I was ordering my tea at the counter and saying hello to Sherry, one of the lovely ladies who works there. It was a slow afternoon so we had a little time to chat with each other and got onto the subject of a fascinating synchronicity that happened earlier that day. Before long we got onto the topic of miracles. She seemed very interested in hearing about the miraculous medal when she noticed the one I was wearing. By this time the only people in the little coffee shop were Sherry, myself, and her co-worker Tom, who was nearby but not engaging in the conversation.

I was concerned that telling the story would take up too much of Sherry's time, but she encouraged me to drop that concern and share anyway. "If someone comes in just pause while I help them and we'll get back to where we left off after I'm done serving them" she said. I took her through the whole story (the one I opened with in this chapter) about the dream I had with the miraculous medal, my mother finding a medal in a used book store, Steve leaving the wheelchair behind, the original story of how the medals came to be, etc. without having one person come into the shop during that time. Her eyes were filled with amazement and she wholeheartedly thanked me for the inspiration she felt from the story.

I reached in my purse and pulled out the little pouch where I keep miraculous medals and asked her to hold out her hand. As I placed the medal in her hand I offered a quick prayer and requested a blessing for her. The energy was buzzing so strong I could feel the electricity moving through our fingers. I looked at Tom and asked "would you like to have a medal as well"? He kindly replied "no, that's okay, I'm good." Sherry was so happy to receive her medal that she reached her arms out, gave me a big hug, and promised to put her medal in a special place.

About two months later, while back at the coffee shop, Tom was serving my tea and said "I put a little something extra on the plate for you." I gleefully thought to myself that it must be a small treat like a cookie, but when I saw a little metal looking object I curiously picked it up and saw that it was a miraculous medal. It wasn't quite like the ones that I give out to people; this one was a little larger and thicker. I surprisingly looked at Tom and said "where did this come from?" He replied "I found it on the floor the other day when I was sweeping; I asked around to see if it belonged to anyone. No one claimed it, so I saved it for you, thought you'd like it after hearing your story about the medal a while back."

As I stood holding the medal it struck me "Tom, in the story that I shared that day do you remember me telling Sherry that the medal that was given to me by my mother was originally found by her in a used book store? Essentially that's where you found this one." We both marveled at the synchronicity of the experience. It almost seemed that I was being reminded of something, no matter how long ago a miracle happens, or where it happens, there are plenty more to go around. That put a little extra skip in my walk that day, and it was much needed too.

Chapter Four

Love Abounds

Love is the strongest force the world possesses, and yet it is the humblest imaginable. ~ **Mahatma Gandhi**

In the Spring of 1995 I heard an amazing story about a woman named Kaye O'Bara and her daughter Edwarda. This is a story of miracles and great love; and how hope never dies. When Edwarda was a teen, some forty years earlier, she had fallen ill and had to be taken to the emergency room due to complications from diabetes. While lying in her hospital bed, she was sliding in and out of consciousness. She said to her mother "Promise you won't leave me, will you, Mommy?" With all her heart Kaye said, "Of course not, I would never leave you, Darling, I promise. And a promise is a promise!" Shortly after that, Edwarda fell into a coma and has been there since that time, so far.

Kaye was a school teacher and left her job to stay by Edwarda's side in the hospital. Edwarda's father remained working to take care of the family's financial needs. At some point, Kaye felt that if she were to leave her in the hospital Edwarda would not survive, and decided to bring her home and take care of her there. The hospital staff tried to discourage her, and the insurance company told Kaye that if she took Edwarda home their medical coverage for her would cease. Still feeling that it was the best thing to do, Kaye followed her intuition and brought Edwarda home. She would now be taking care of her full time.

A few years later Kaye's husband gently told her that he had a feeling about something; that he would be leaving soon. He said that he felt he was going to pass on and do his work helping them from the other side. Shortly after that he had a fatal heart attack and indeed passed on.

Kaye was now left to find a way to support Edwarda, who was still in a coma, by herself. Subsequently there were many gifts that had shown up over the years. To help ease some of Kaye's hardships, there were numerous miracles that had manifested in her life. For example, the family doctor continued medical care for Edwarda and made home visits at no charge. Kaye was able to stay by Edwarda's bedside and work by phone requesting donations of autographed baseballs, bats, footballs, etc. from famous sports figures. She would then have them sold at auctions to raise money to pay for Edwarda's insulin and other expenses.

Of all the wonderful offerings that had come about so far, none could match what was about to happen that would further the mission of Edwarda and Kaye. I should mention that word had gotten out about Edwarda's years of lying comatose in her bed at home. Letters and cards of support had shown up from time to time, however, there were also people who believed that Edwarda should be "put out of her misery" and cut off from her life support system that had been set up at their home. There was even a drive by shooting that occurred to prove their conviction of what they believed. Fortunately Kaye and Edwarda were not struck by the bullets that penetrated their home.

What many may not have known was that Edwarda had some unusual circumstances that sustained her beyond the life support known for a coma patient. For a number of years she has been in the last stage of coma. This is the stage a patient reaches before they finally attain an awakened state. She also had not ceased her menstruation all those years, which is unheard of for someone in a coma that long. In addition to Edwarda's intravenous support, she could also be fed by mouth.

One late night, while sleeping, Kaye awoke and went to Edwarda's room to check on her. At first, Kaye was startled by what she feared was an intruder in Edwarda's room. There was a very bright light hovering next to Edwarda's bed. Kaye trembled at the thought of anything happening to her daughter. Suddenly the light began to communicate with her, letting her know that she need not be afraid; it was Mother Mary who had stood before her.

Relieved, yet still somewhat overwhelmed by this miraculous visitation, Kaye and Mother Mary briefly spent time communicating with one another. Kaye asked why Edwarda had fallen comatose for so many years. Mary explained that Edwarda had chosen this state as her means of expressing her purpose on earth, and further explained that Edwarda's mission is to create awareness and to bring comfort, hope, and compassion to those in need. "Edwarda choose this?" asked Kaye. Mary replied "It's always a choice." This helped to give Kaye a better understanding of how things came to be the way they are, but she still wanted to know why things were so strained financially. Mary shared with Kaye that she had been very creative in her endeavors to meet her financial responsibilities and that her creativity had served them well.

The visitations continued, and more miracles came along the way. Kaye had been born color blind. Soon after the visitations with Mother Mary began she was given the gift of seeing color, which she joyfully embraced. On another occasion someone showed up at her door and gave Kaye a rose bush to plant. She immediately planted it in her back yard. When Mary appeared to say "plant the rose bush in the front yard for all to see" Kaye moved it to the front yard. When the roses started to bloom the bush miraculously created 5 different colored blooms on the one bush, with No Thorns.

There is another incident that is noteworthy. Kaye had found out about someone who offered loans; returnable by monthly payments. She had faithfully made the monthly payments for quite some time, when one day the man who came by for the collections stopped coming to her door. Kaye assumed that the loan must have been paid off and satisfied. A couple of years later the same man appeared at her door demanding full payment of the rest of the loan. She was shocked and didn't understand why, after all that time, he was back at her doorstep. He explained that he had been in jail all that time and had just been released; now he wanted the rest of the payments upfront within the hour. Kaye explained that she could not possibly come up with that kind of money on such short notice. He threatened to hurt Edwarda if she didn't have it within the hour and said he would be back to collect the money, then left.

In desperation, Kaye looked up to the heavens telling God to bring the $600 that was owed right now, even if he had to bust a whole in the ceiling to bring it down to her. Not a second later there was a knock at the door. She quickly answered in hopes that who ever it was would be quick so that she could get back to figuring out how she was going to come up with the money. When she opened the door, there stood a kind man with an envelope saying that he had heard about Edwarda's illness and wanted to bring a card by for her. Kaye thanked him, accepted the envelope, and apologized for having to rush back to what she was doing. After closing the door she opened the envelope and found exactly $600 cash inside.

Without haste, Kaye opened the door to see if she could call out to the kind man but he was nowhere to be seen. She asked her neighbors, who were working in the yard across the street, if they knew which way the man went that was just at her door. They said that the only thing they saw was Kaye opening the door, talking as if there was someone there, then they saw her reach her hand out into thin air as if she was taking something, and then saw her go back inside and close the door. They never saw a man there talking with her. Needless to say Kaye's prayer had been answered, the loan was paid off, and she was in great appreciation for the mystery man who brought the gift and the answered prayer.

By the time I had heard about Edwarda's story she was in her early to mid forties, and had been comatose for most of her life; miracles were still abundantly surprising everyone. I heard that Dr Wayne Dyer had written a book about Edwarda and Kaye, and I felt strongly compelled to have Kaye share the story on the air. The book is titled "A Promise is a Promise," published by Hay House. Dr Dyer is donating all profits to the O'Bara family for the care of Edwarda. Their website is EdwardaOBara.com. I decided to invite her on my *Miraculous In Everyday* segment in hopes that the story would help to inspire others as it did me. The publisher put me in contact with Kaye and we spoke on the phone to talk about dates for scheduling the interview. I was so happy that she was interested in coming on the show.

Kaye was just as loving as I imagined her to be, and very accommodating.

We both agreed to check our schedules and report back the next day. That night I had a dream about Edwarda and Kaye. I dreamed that I showed up at their home. There was a very large group of people showing up, most of them bringing food. It appeared that there was a celebration of some kind going on in their home. I walked into the kitchen and saw quite a few dishes in the sink. I felt that Kaye needed help with things so I decided to roll up my sleeves and start washing dishes. Then I noticed that the water in the sink turned to wine. That is all I remember about the dream, somehow I knew it would be a good idea to share about the dream with Kaye.

When we spoke on the phone the next day we got the date set for the interview. Once that was squared away I asked if she had time to chat a moment further so that I could describe a dream I had about her and Edwarda. Intrigued, she let me know that she was very interested in hearing about it. As I shared the details of the dream she was astounded at the coincidence of the timing and explained that Edwarda's birthday would be in a couple of weeks where many people were expected to show up for the celebration. Kaye said that the year before there were nearly 200 people who had come to their home, some even traveled from as far away as Canada, and many of them brought food. She felt that maybe the dream was a sign that I was supposed to be there. I was excited at the idea of coming to visit, nothing would make me happier than to meet dear Edwarda and Kaye in person. I explained that I was not sure if I could pull together enough funds for the air fare in time, but I would see what I could do.

The interview was more heartwarming and impacting than I could have imagined. I was so grateful for the time she spent sharing the story on the air. I knew that the listeners got a lot out of the message of love she so beautifully conveyed. I asked how Edwarda was doing and Kaye said that she was by her side and very much a part of the interview. I had no doubt that her energy was right there with us.

It was a few days before Edwarda's birthday and I still did not have enough money to cover the air fare. I had hopes that the right amount of money would be available, but time was running out and a decision had to be made. I picked up the phone to let Kaye know that I would not be able to make it after all. When I talked with her, she was disappointed but understood. She mentioned that there was a lot of work to do in preparation for all the people who were coming, so I let her get back to her list of things to do.

I could not let go of the feeling that I was still supposed to be there. The rest of the day I continued to feel those feelings until an out-of-the-blue thought hit me like a ton of bricks ... "I have an airline pass that I have not used yet!" Yes! It was from an occasion where I was bumped from a flight some months ago and the airline gave me an extra pass as a courtesy; how did I not remember this until now? New hope had arrived! I got right on the phone to see if I could schedule a flight. The reservation agent explained that the time I wished to schedule my flight was during spring break, and the rules prohibited use of the type of pass I had for that time period.

"Well, I gave it my best shot" I thought. "Sure wish it could have worked out." I started to go on with my day and then stopped in my tracks. "I'm not giving up!" I got right back on the phone and called the reservation number again. A sweet voice answered; this time I shared from my heart what I was traveling for and told her about Edwarda's birthday; who she is, and how much it would mean to me to make it there for her celebration.

It was almost like the voice of an angel ... "Here's how you do it." She started telling me how I could work with stand-by and still make it on the plane with the airline pass that I had. I could hardly contain myself and thanked the angel on the other end of the phone with whole hearted delight.

I made it on the plane and arrived in Miami without a hitch, but time was of the essence. My dear friend Matt, who lives in Miami, picked me up from the airport and drove me all the way to Kaye and Edwarda's home. I invited him to join the festivities, and he was very happy to join in. As we approached the front door of their home, I noticed a very strong scent of roses. I remembered that Kaye had been given a rose bush to plant in her front yard. I looked around to see if that might be where the rose scent was coming from. There was, what looked like, a rose bush; but there was not a single bloom in sight. I could not see any other plant life around that would put out such a beautiful aroma.

We knocked on the door and were greeted by a lovely elderly woman. We introduced ourselves and asked if we made it in time for the birthday song. With a great big smile she said "You've made it just in time, they're lighting the candles for Edwarda's cake right now." I asked where I could find Kaye and she directed me to Edwarda's room. The house was filled with bright cheery people, lots of food, and great anticipation for an auspicious celebration. I explained that Kaye wanted me to find her when I arrived. The lovely guide called out across the crowd of people and said "Kaye, your friend Claire is here." "Oh Claire, bring her here to Edwarda" it was Kaye's voice but I couldn't see her through the crowd of people. My guide grabbed my hand as she waded through the many friends who had come to see Edwarda, bringing me across the room to her bedside. My heart was so happy to see Edwarda; I felt so filled with joy.

The air was overflowing with anticipation; the light beaming from everyone's eyes would have made one think they had landed in heaven. And Edwarda seemed so alert, and peacefully connected to the energy of the room. It was almost as if I could feel her heartbeat in mine. I looked across the bed and there stood Dr. Wayne Dyer beaming at Edwarda much the same as I was. I lost sight of Matt; he was still behind the many smiling faces that were huddled together in the packed full room. Then the room began to burst with song as a large cake with flaming candles, carried by a tiny woman with a big heart, made its way through the crowd. It was Kaye! She brought the cake up to Edwarda's bed, then, when the song was finished, everyone inhaled a deep breath and blew out the candles. I don't think I have ever heard the birthday song sung quite the way I heard it that day, every word sung with pure gusto and exuberance!

It was so clear that Edwarda was showing signs of enjoying herself. I had nothing to compare by, being the first time ever seeing her, but anyone in the room would have agreed. There was a revealing presence about her that let it be known how connected she was to the celebration.

Kaye passed the cake over to a friend to start serving it up in the kitchen, and introduced me to Dr. Dyer. I had read his books for many years, and was very happy to meet him. The work he has done has contributed so much positive change in so many lives.

I met a lot of wonderful people that day; each one of them with a beautiful story of how their lives have been affected by the inspiring experience of knowing Edwarda and Kaye. It soon became evening, I decided to bring a few lingering empty paper plates and cups to the kitchen to help tidy up from the feast. While tossing the paper goods in a nearby trash bag I remembered the part of my dream where I was helping out with the dishes. Noticing that the sink was quite full of things waiting to be washed I rolled up my sleeves to begin digging in. Kaye entered the room chuckling about how I flew all the way from Texas to help out with the dishes; she too remembered that part of my dream.

As I began to reach the bottom of the bucket that was in the sink I found a puddle of wine. "This is so funny" I thought, there was water that had turned to wine while cleaning dishes in my dream. Only I'm sure in this case, the wine came from glasses that had wine in them and made their way into the bucket.

Things were winding down and I knew that I needed to let Matt start heading back toward his end of town, it was time to say our good byes. Kaye asked if I would be in town the next day, she wanted me to come back where we could spend a little quiet time together. I was hoping there would be time for that, but didn't want to impose in case Kaye had other obligations. I happily agreed to return the next afternoon.

The next day greeted me with colorful rays of sunshine dancing through the window. The hotel I was staying in wasn't far from the shoreline. There was plenty of time before we were due to arrive at Kaye and Edwarda's home, so my friend Roland offered to swing by the beach on our way. Roland, like Matt, is a friend of mine who lives in Miami. I met them both at a conference in Denver a few years ago. We found that we had a lot in common and quickly became friends. Our ties remained over the years even though we didn't connect that often.

It seemed that someone had ordered the perfect weather for a walk on the beach that day. I especially wanted to pay the beach a visit so that I could throw a Miraculous Medal into the ocean. As we strolled, I was paying close attention to an inner prompting of the right place to stop in prayer, and then toss the medal in the ocean. I found the most inviting energy and set forth a prayer for Kaye and Edwarda; for healing to manifest in the lives of all who needed it, and for peace to prevail on Earth. I envisioned Light filling and surrounding the area. Then, I threw the medal as far into the ocean as I could reach. We both commented on how strong the loving, peaceful energy felt at that moment.

Then Roland began to get excited. "Look Claire, it's a stone that looks like people"...he picked it up and handed it to me. As we gazed upon the sandstone we were speechless. It was a smooth, sort of bas-relief, sculpture of Mother Mary holding what looked like baby Jesus. This appeared to be a natural formation, not something man made. We both stood in awe of such a find. "This is really Amazing Roland, you should take this home and put it in a special place" I said. He insisted that I keep it and said that he felt it was supposed to go with me. Then I looked down at my feet and saw a perfectly shaped sea shell that had a perfectly shaped baby sea shell nestled in its lip. It didn't take but a moment to notice a second one like it, with a baby sea shell nestled right at its lip, only a different color and a little smaller. The shells seemed to imitate the sandstone of Mary holding the infant Jesus.

By this time Roland seemed to be beside himself. "Claire, look around you" he said. I did a quick scan of the immediate area of the beach. "Do you see anymore shells or stones shaped like these?" said Roland. As far as I could see there wasn't another shell or stone like the ones we had just found. With passion in his eyes he said "That's right Claire, there aren't any others like these. I've been on this beach many times, and it is very rare to find a whole sea shell here, much less with another whole shell lodged in its lip. The odds of finding one are astronomical and even greater odds to find two of them as you have." I didn't realize the enormity until he pointed it out to me. But he was right. Resting right in the very place we were standing were three representations of Mother Mary holding baby Jesus.

As we made our way back to the car Roland and I kept careful watch for anything else that could resemble the three miraculous pieces we had just found ... nothing came close. All of the other shells on the beach were in pieces; none were still in their original whole state. I don't think there is a lot to say when an event happens like this. You just take it in and experience it. We don't always know why things like this happen. Sometimes just being with the whole experience brings forth an understanding in layers. Even years later one can be left wondering "what was that all about ... a conformation ... a sign?" The mystery sometimes feels like the very essence of heaven undefined. I accept the gifts with humble gratitude and await opportunities to work with the gifts when they can be of service.

We arrived at Edwarda and Kaye's home just in time. Kaye greeted us at the door and offered us both a big hug and a hearty smile, then invited us back to see Edwarda in her room. The TV was on and Edwarda's head was pointed in that direction with eyes slightly cracked open. "I leave the TV on for her to watch when her favorite shows are on" said Kaye. She explained that although Edwarda is comatose, she is considered to be in the last stage where it's almost, but not quite, like being awake.

People around the world who have experienced pain and suffering have reported that Edwarda has appeared to them, often taking their pain and leaving them with a spiritual sense of comfort and peace. I remember Kaye telling a story about a woman from South America who had heard about Edwarda and came to see her. The woman was told by her doctor that she had a brain tumor and would be having surgery the following week after her visit with them. When she arrived, Kaye sat her next to Edwarda to visit for a while. Then the woman placed Edwarda's hand on her head for a few moments. When it was time to leave she thanked them both for allowing her to be there and promised to stay in touch.

A few days later Kaye heard back from their South American visitor excitedly sharing that her doctor ordered one more MRI before the surgery and discovered the large tumor was completely gone; nowhere to be found. A week later workers showed up at Kaye's door saying that they came to put new carpet in, compliments of her friend from South America.

It was a real joy to spend more time with Edwarda and Kaye. It is truly a humbling experience to sit with Edwarda and recognize who this beautiful soul is. On the outside you see a woman having been comatose for more than four decades. During the time we were there Edwarda would make a noise to let Kaye know that she was hungry. When her position became uncomfortable, her mother would adjust her pillow and the sounds of discomfort would stop. Kaye even mentioned that sometimes Edwarda expresses her emotions when there was something she didn't like or when she needed to be turned to another position. I remember Kaye sharing that there are people who say Edwarda is a vegetable and ask why she keeps hanging on to her instead of just "pulling the plug" so to speak. They aren't there to see just how alive Edwarda really is.

Beyond that, there are almost no words to describe how impacting it is to witness such service in action. The loving sweetness of the environment would make anyone feel at home.

Roland and I knew that Kaye would appreciate hearing about our time at the beach. We told her what happened that morning when I threw the Miraculous Medal in the ocean, and how we found the sandstone and sea shells. As Kaye held the sandstone, she could clearly see the shape of Mother Mary and the infant Jesus. She looked at me and said "Claire, you are supposed to show this to people, keep this." Then she showed me a small, oval, silver colored medal with an image of a woman kneeling, reaching up to a bare cross, on what seemed to be a hill. The words "The Matrix" were printed at the bottom. I found out that the woman in the medal is Mother Mary. On the other side of the medal was an image of two interlinked hearts that appeared to be weeping or bleeding.

Kaye said that some time ago Mother Mary asked her to place some of these medals in Edwarda's hand and Mary would bless the medals. "This medal is for you" she said, as she placed one in my hand. It made my heart sing just holding it as I expressed my appreciation for her sharing it with me.

Kaye asked me to sing Mary's Lullaby for Edwarda as she went to answer the door. They get visitors often, and their home is always open to those who want to come by. While I sang, I could feel a sisterly connection with Edwarda and gave thanks for the experience. My sense is that much of Edwarda resides in the higher dimensions where she does most of the work she is here to do.

This would be a good time to share about a dream I had with Edwarda shortly after I returned to Houston. Here is what I remember from the dream … I was sitting next to Edwarda while she lay in bed. Only, instead of being in a coma, she was sitting up in bed, fully awake, younger, and vibrant. She seemed to be busy at work with different tasks; reading letters that had been sent to her and other similar things. I felt a strong family connection with her, almost like she was an older sister I had always known. Even though she was awake and fully active, I was thinking about the hard places she must be in while comatose with the physical pain she must be enduring. It seemed that this was sort of a dual reality for her. It felt as though I was concerned for her third dimensional experience of the physical state she was in. I asked her "how do you do it?" Meaning how do you endure so much, for so many years? Then, I was shown her 'other self' in her comatose state lying there, and I could hear her telepathically saying "It is in my hair." At this point the dream no longer felt like a dream, it became lucid. In reality, Edwarda's hair is very long, way past her hips and kept in a braid, and was still that way in the dream. What I seem to instinctively understand from her reply, was that the length of her hair also represents the length of her endurance, strength, and spiritually; which is very long and endless. She truly is just fine.

Kaye entered the room just as I had finished singing and I knew that it was time to get back to the hotel and get packed for a very early morning flight back to Houston. I had just remembered to ask about the rose bush she had spoken of that has five different colored blooms and no thorns. She said that before I got to her house yesterday quite a few people had taken the blooms as mementos to bring home with them. This is something that she makes available to anyone who wants them. "Lets go outside and I will show you the bush" she said. I took one last glance at Edwarda, gently touched her hand, and thanked her for all of the service that she is doing for humanity. I knew we would see each other again.

Kaye led us outside to see the miraculous rose bush. Indeed, all of the blooms were gone, so she offered to let us have some of the leaves, which we happily accepted. I felt as if I had already received a rose the day before when I could smell the strong scent of roses as I approached her front door. There have been other occasions when the scent of roses has shown up while there were no roses in sight. Mother Mary has been known to bring the scent when she is letting her presence be known. Many people have spoken of this type of experience.

As Roland and I leaned closer to the large bush, we could see that there were no thorns on the stems. There were no pluck marks where thorns could have previously been either. The stems were smooth and green from top to bottom.

We each shared a big embrace and a brief moment of looking into each others eyes, no words were necessary. Roland and I waved as we were pulling away from Kaye's drive way and let out a thankful sigh as we were leaving. Sad to leave, and happy we came.

Chapter Five

Where there is Hope – there is Action

The future is not some place we are going to but one we are creating. The paths to it are not found but made. ~ **John Schaar**

We live in a powerful time, one that few human beings before us have ever experienced. Ancient traditions suggest that something really big will happen during our time in history. Contrary to the interpretations of various media sources, the prophecies of the ancient cultures have not spoken of the world itself ending; they have only taught that the world as we know it will enter a time of great change.

What will we create? What will we bring to this new world? We are capable of amazing things, and are being given a choice not to wait for the future, and all that it brings, but to help birth the future into to being.

* * *

As I drove to my friend Sandy's house, I was excited to catch up with her after her magical trip to New Zealand. I had really missed her and looked forward to exchanging the warm hugs we always greeted each other with. She met many wonderful people on her journey and had remarkable adventures along the way. The bonds that were formed made way for a few of her new friends to visit her in Houston. To celebrate their arrival, Sandy planned a special gathering at her home where all her local friends could meet her distinctive visitors from abroad.

The evening was warm and a bit humid, not unusual for Houston. However, there was a hint of something different in the air not easy to describe. It left an almost curious feeling of what it would bring. I arrived at Sandy's home with a platter full of organic strawberries and chocolate dipping sauce to tantalize dessert lovers after the delicious dinner that was prepared. Sandy joyfully introduced each of us, one by one. The room was filled with festive music, laughter and fun stories. It was as if we all had known each other our whole lives.

It was soon time to join together for a specially prepared guided meditation that Sandy had planned. We all found a comfortable seat in chairs and pillows on the floor. Sandy has a wonderful gift with words, and uses her deep wisdom and intuition to guide the visualization process when facilitating group meditations. She opened with a relaxing voice making way for a loving affirmation of harmony for humanity and Earth. I settled in listening to the sound of her hypnotic voice and quickly went into a deep state of relaxation. I could feel myself connecting with that place within that always brings me new revelations.

Once we were complete with the beautiful energy and calming space of peaceful meditation, Sandy put out the invitation for those who wanted to share their experience. Everyone commented on how grateful they were for the tranquil feeling the visualization brought them.

After the sharing portion was over, one of the ladies from New Zealand started a conversation about the changes that humanity and Earth would be going through in the coming years. Many of the people there that night were aware of the changes on some level. The conversation started light; however for some, it shifted to a heaviness of great concern. I listened, in an attempt to hold a nurturing space, knowing that it was healing for them to express their feelings. Several others joined in who tearfully spoke of a bleak looking future that had no promise of getting better.

Although Sandy and I did not share the same perception, my heart went out to them for the pain that they felt.

It was then that I began to hear the inner voice of Mother Mary speaking to me. I felt the immense loving presence of her energy reaching out from the depths of her heart. Her presence seemed to fill the room as she spoke her message, "Remember - Where there is hope, there is action!" It was very strong, very direct, and she very clearly wanted the message to be shared with the group. I felt somewhat choked up from the great love that I had just felt coming from Mother Mary and had to quickly compose myself. I asked the group if I could share a message with them. They seemed relieved, as if they somehow knew one was coming.

As I shared the message, I could feel the thick layer of hopelessness lift from the air in the room. I explained that the message came from Mother Mary, and although it was short, it was packed with wisdom and loving direction. I believe she was letting us know that no matter how challenging things may appear in our lives, we can always hold hope for things to move beyond whatever challenges may be afoot. We can gather ourselves and move forward, doing our part in relation to all the opportunities available to us. With Hope, there is motivation to take Action; both of which help to create the energy for a brighter world. Action helps to build momentum, and when there appears to be no answer in sight, solutions emerge and rise like the phoenix out of the ashes.

There was a very hearty sigh of relief in the room as the tears turned into smiles. It was my hope that each of us carries Mary's message in our hearts to remind us of the miraculous energy hope holds for us, and the alchemy that occurs when we take action for a new world; a new creation of heaven on Earth. Many of us have begun to understand the astonishing effects of the power of love and of using our intentions to create new possibilities. When coupled with action, we have an even more powerful force to work with.

It is true that we are all going through a period of massive transformation personally, collectively, and planetarily. Systems and structures that many of us have been accustomed to for most of our lives are in the process of momentous change. In some cases, they are destabilizing, only to introduce an entirely new era that is now emerging. Even our climate is looking very different than what we are used to, and will continue to change substantially for the next few years or more. Another area that will have vast sweeping effects on all of us is the revelation that the people of our world are not alone in the Universe. At the point we are at now, there is no turning back. Forward is where we are headed, and new possibilities form from the change that is now underway, allowing the fertile soil of creativity to blossom even further.

The only way to make sense out of change is to plunge into it, move with it, and join the dance. ~ **Alan Watts**

There are many who are using their awareness to be more prepared for the coming changes that will occur in all areas of our lives; physically, mentally, emotionally, and spiritually. I encourage you to pattern your preparedness according to the guidance you receive from your inner connection with God, the Source of All That Is. Tune into your intuition and inner wisdom, and listen to what you feel in your heart – do not rely on your reasoning power alone. It is from within that you open the doors to a strong heart for the unprecedented changes of our time.

While moving through the changes, we can call upon grace in every situation. Hope will bring people together to serve in ways that bring deeper meaning into the human experience. New ways of joining together in service for the personal and collective good will come forth. It has been said that hope sees the invisible, feels the intangible, and achieves the impossible. Courageous hope; a hope that knows no bounds and opens the way to the kind of courage that propels us past thresholds and obstacles is what we are rising to.

There will be creative new ways to work with the changes by sharing what is available, discovering new systems and creating new designs, and applying healing in ways that had only been dreamed of, or not noticed, until now. New and renewable resources come alive, while ingenuity paves the way for implementation. The awareness that there are always possibilities fuels a stronger sense of the miracles that await us. Challenges will be seen as opportunities to be creative as we allow our intentions, and our will, to lift old paradigms to new ways of being and living.

Heart connections will help create a very new structure. Love is what will fuel this new structure, and love is what will sustain it. For those who have felt downtrodden, they will discover that acts of loving service will bring a new sense of thriving and newfound happiness. In this time of acceleration, many of us are noticing that we are being stretched to reach deeper into places within ourselves that are still left to be healed. This strengthens us to use our inner wisdom and love as an approach for every aspect of our lives. The more heart-centered energy there is on this planet, the more empowered we are to better accommodate the greater changes in the world.

Gregg Braden, author of ***The Isaiah Affect, Deep Truth,*** and many other paradigm changing books, talks about how Scientists have acknowledged an invisible force of energy around us, known as "the field," that connects all things. Albert Einstein said that this field is the sole governing agency of the particle. Today's scientists agree that Earth's magnetic fields are weakening quickly. As the magnetics of our poles decrease, Braden says that our body's rhythms are tuned to the heart beat and pulse of the Earth, and will continually shift to match Mother Earth's fundamental increase of her pulse, which has been accelerating for quite some time. Since we are all connected through a field of energy, we can intentionally infuse this energy with the love we focus on from our hearts, consciously contributing to a more loving, compassionate, peaceful world.

Miracles are not contrary to nature, but only contrary to what we know about nature. ~ **Saint Augustine**

There is great power in living consciously, and in holding a new vision of what our world can be, and is becoming. Marianne Williamson says it well in her book, *A Return to Love*, "Living out of our vision is more powerful than living out of our circumstance." The support to live that vision with unwavering strength, is not a learning process, it is a remembering process that emerges from within us. The loving presence we bring to the world spreads like rose pedals along the path – we are both the traveler and the path. As we awaken to the understanding that we create what we believe, we start believing in the things that we want to create.

With the goal of celebrating and helping one another, even the smallest efforts can yield miraculous results. I read an article that shows the power people possess when they pull together and use their creative abilities in the face of adversity. The article covered a story reported by the CBS Evening News of a human chain made up of 30 people who were rescuing five beachgoers from a riptide in Bloomington Point Beach, Prince Edward Island. The five swimmers were enjoying the afternoon in the water when suddenly the rip yanked their footing out from under them and pulled them, quickly, and without warning, into deep water. The swimmers could have drowned, but bystanders linked their arms, formed a long line and, after nearly an hour, managed to pull every one of them to safety. Strangers and friends pulled together, connected, arm by arm, and found the strength to rescue all those people. The courage to unite was stronger than the fear of the challenge they faced.

Just imagine a world where this type of creative, loving, intuitive, innovative and powerful force grows in even greater abundance to bring solutions to many of the challenges already at hand. There is an African proverb that says "If you want to go quickly, go alone. If you want to go far, go together." Truly a new sight will awaken in people from every part of the world. The miraculous spirit of united community, compassion, and service, will emerge in amazing ways. People will share their skills, talents, gifts, energy and resources to give rise to the new world they choose to create.

This quote, author unknown, really speaks to where we are headed as humanity continues to awaken and unite, *"The darkness of our world awaits you - not to engulf you, but to be transformed by you.*" It is so very important to remember this as we meet, with open hearts, what ever dark places are left. As we compassionately support the transformation of those dark places back to their true nature of love, the very essence of who we are as a people is restored more fully as well. We will be working to shed Light on many things that are up for change with our open hearts, and anchor in new choices of how to live and be in the world.

There is no adverse condition that cannot be righted with the power of intent and the right use of will...Where the will is established, a way will present itself that is clear, concise and forthcoming. As compassion and authenticity continue to increase, humanity will discover the courage and willingness to heal the environment and the world. Abundance, health and joy will replace scarcity, poverty and fear. ~ **Gaia (Mother Earth), as shared through Pepper Lewis**

As more and more people step into a higher vision of themselves, and of each other, old paradigms of war, control, or separation of any kind, will give way to a new way, and higher way, of being. Dr Bruce Lipton, author of *Biology of Belief*, talks about how crisis ignites evolution. He says that the challenges the world faces today are actually signs that change is imminent; and we are about to face our evolution. We will find meaning in whatever crises arise and begin to trust that whatever happens next is happening in some form of service to our own evolution. Change is the natural order of things, and is also a way of getting our attention. In this way, change can be thought of as an ally. Compassionate, conscious acknowledgment of the transition we are all going through is essential as well. Gently holding ourselves in the softness of our own hearts through any uncomfortable passages of the transformation will help us adapt more easily.

The spiritual evolution and restoration of our wholeness has already begun, and yet, has never been apart from us, only temporarily covered up by the fog of the stories we have told ourselves. We are stepping into a new level of sovereignty with ourselves and unity with all sentient life. It is a great time to be alive and to be here on Earth. It is truly a time for remembering, rediscovery, deliverance, truth; a time of becoming the very things that we would like to experience in the world. Creation indeed loves creating itself. A dear friend once said – "Let's live life and enjoy the ride, for it is truly what we make of it."

Chapter Six

Each Journey Brings a New Dawn

Each of us has had a story where inklings, gut feelings, or a dream has led to a path very different from what we might have imagined in one form or another. Each story I have ever heard has been inspiring, beautiful, and unique. I would like to share one such story that began as early as the year 1990. I was shown, through dreams and meditations, that I would be hosting and producing programs to help inspire human potential and offer new ways of thinking about the world we live in.

I was first led to start working as a traffic and news anchor/producer on local radio stations. Through some pretty miraculous events, the news radio work evolved into producing and hosting a national radio talk show on the Wisdom Network for Wisdom Radio (later to become Lime Radio) which aired on Sirius Satellite Radio, coast to coast in the U.S. and Canada.

There was much hard work and many synchronicities that went into the manifestation of this program. I give a lot of credit and gratitude to my friend Scott who played a major role in mentoring me in the beginning, and who was responsible for getting the show that we hosted together on the air. Our show was called "Wisdom Today" which aired on the Wisdom Network. We were still in the developmental stages of the show and had a good deal of correspondence going on with the staff at the Wisdom Media offices. Daniel, one of the managers, had been in close contact with me discussing details about the production of the show. We both spoke about how our hearts were filled with hope about the potential that each of the shows had to support and inspire the listeners. I felt that the message that Mother Mary had given me a while back, "Where there is hope, there is action," beautifully spoke to the sentiment that Daniel and I expressed to each other, so I shared the brief message from Mary as a quote in one of my emails to him. This was the message I have already talked about in chapter 5. I knew that Daniel was very busy, not only with my show, but with several others that would be launching at the same time. I did not want to assume he would want to hear the long story of my experience as a Marian visionary, so I simply shared the beautiful quote without the details of origin.

We launched the show with great success. Everything flowed; and we could finally relax a little more knowing that the program was well on its mission. By the third day that we were on the air one new piece showed up, the announcer that normally introduced us tossed the show to us with one simple sentence …"Where there is hope, there is action … and now, Wisdom Today." As it turned out Daniel liked the message from Mother Mary so much that it became the "bumper" to our show. I did not even know he had chosen it until the moment it was first spoken on the air. It had been quite some time since Mother Mary had first shared that message with me back at Sandy's home. Now Mary would be sharing it with listeners across the nation each time we were on the air with our daily show. My eyes filled with tears and my heart filled with joy after hearing the announcer speak those words. The whole experience was a wonderful confirmation of how strong Mother Mary's presence was in the work we were doing on the air.

Our beloved founder and owner of the network, Bill Turner, had passed on not long after our show first aired. It would be almost two years from the launch of our show that the network, Wisdom Radio, would move to replays, and sadly discontinue live programming. A month before the announcement that this would be happening I had a dream about spearheading a new show, one that would take the work to a whole new level.

The Dream Continues

My new show, "It's All Good," was born in a dream. As I slept, I was shown that I would be interviewing luminaries that many of us have never heard of, as well as having conversations with popular authors offering advice that listeners would be hearing for the first time. In the dream, I went to the Wisdom Media office. There was a new level of the building that was being constructed in a very beautiful setting, and I could feel the network changing and expanding. I had to gently walk up the stairs to the new level because the steps were still being built and were quite delicate. Once I made it to the top of the stairs, I walked to the windows and gazed out at hills which were covered with red carpets. I felt a large number of people were expected to show up on these red carpets—everything was ready and waiting for a special event.

Instantly, I was outside on the grounds where the red carpet contrasted beautifully with the green velvet rolling hills. People showed up and made themselves comfortable. At that moment, I realized that they were anticipating hearing new programs that would be launching. They were there to get practical tools to help them apply personal growth theories and wisdom to their families and workplaces as they create more sustainable, healthy, lifestyles. As the red carpets filled up, I felt the gratitude coming from the listeners. And I felt my own gratitude for this wonderful work.

I had a sense that this new show would air on a Saturday and would have a strong emphasis on the great transformation that humanity is embarking upon. As we all experience these transformations, we need to maintain a healthy personal life, as well as healthy families, as we work toward building a new peaceful world community. To do this means healing the simplest parts of our own lives in order to heal larger world issues. Everything we do for ourselves and our own healing raises the group consciousness and leaves a trail for others to follow. I knew that this show would be a resource that not only feeds the soul, but explores in-depth practical tips, offering the necessary ongoing tools to address and heal different areas of life like parenting, or relationship, workplace, environmental, health and wellness issues, as well as bring us together as a global community.

A month later, when the announcement came that the Wisdom Network would no longer have live programming, I already knew that there would be a new generation of shows that would surface, and the opportunity to still be of service through radio would make its way again. I focused my attention on this awareness and surrendered the outcome to the heavens. Even though I was not sure how it would happen, I knew without a doubt that I would be hosting a new show, and it would manifest at the right time, in the right place. I believed that what you see, feel, and focus on with passion will be drawn to you. I gave up focusing on how; that's the work of the Universe, I just continued to focus on the end result and held onto my vision.

A good amount of time had passed, might have been nearly a year, when I received an email that was sent to all the prior hosts of Wisdom Radio. It came from a new media group that bought the Wisdom Network, and would now be called Lime Radio. They invited each of us to contact them and share ideas for new shows. I called the Lime Radio office and told them I had an idea for a show. They seemed delighted that I was interested in submitting my idea and asked me to send my proposal.

I shared much of what came from the dream that I had about the new show. I knew from the dream that there would be a whole host of listeners with challenges who would benefit from what the program would have to offer … worn-out parents juggling work and family; stressed-out couples wanting better relationships; discouraged environmental stewards, troubled teens, and disappointed people in the workplace who wanted to hear new ideas on how to use timeless principles from the great masters and understand how to translate them into practical support for everyday life. Inspiration for creating a future of a unified global community would also grow out of the conversations we would have on the air.

A week later, I was contacted by Laura, the operations manager, who said "We love your concept. We want the show; how about having it premiere on Saturdays with replays throughout the week?" It was one of those shivery confirmations.

If you look back through your life, you will see things you envisioned to manifest, and if you look for the magic, you will see the good things you have already brought into manifestation. You can use your successes as the foundation to manifest your new dreams through recognition and gratitude. No matter how small your success is, it's the beginning of living your dream. Stay connected to your own passion and vision, and trust the process as it unfolds.

The Lime Network blessed the air waves on Sirius Satellite Radio for nearly two years, and then gracefully went off the air. I was in the company of around 20 wonderful hosts on the network, and an amazing staff; every one of us put our hearts and souls in the work. The time spent hosting and producing the show was a pure joy and blessing in my life, and the guests that I had on the show were the angels who championed positive change in the world.

When Wisdom Radio first went on the air, it was the only network that was completely devoted to body, mind, spirit, and earth programming. Lime Radio took the helm not long after that, and now, several years later, there are hundreds of shows and hosts on other networks focusing on the same type of content, carrying the work even further. I am elated to know that the work continues in many forms and in many venues. And the people who tune in, who contribute on the air with their calls, sharing wisdom and offering important questions that need to be asked; they are taking the evolution of this world to the next level, a level that cannot be reckoned with.

In time, each of us completes one story or experience, benefiting from what we have learned and shared, and then move on to a new chapter. Knowing this I stay tuned within and explore the many possibilities for the next part of my own journey, where ever that may lead, or that I feel most drawn to next. The road is full of surprises. Remembrances of other soul promptings are surfacing and the gestation of those seedlings are making themselves known. I find that when I take delight in the mystery, the outcome feels more alive and worthwhile. Nudge on, dear world, I embrace each new dawn.

Chapter Seven

Artistry of a New World

The Creator of the universe, who has ordered the stars and the heavens and the earth, has a plan for your life. You are not a random act. You are not here by chance, but by design. You are destined for greatness that begins with your believing in your own destiny. ~ **Mary Manin Morrissey**

It was a day that started out like most any day; a short meditation and a deep sense of gratitude for the early morning rays of golden sunshine peeking through the window shade. August is a beautiful time of year in Houston; it is also one of the hottest times of the year. Each morning the thirsty plants on my balcony greeted me with gratitude for their daily drink of water. There was a long list of things I had planned to accomplish that day ... ironing (who irons anymore), cleaning out the veggie bin in the fridge; answering emails, researching material for my radio show, writing and recording the show's promos, etc. But for some reason it felt like there was something else that was calling for my attention. It was a faint inner whisper that was lingering through the morning. I had to stop for a moment to really hear what the message was trying to convey..."The Weather Channel...storm."

I reached for the remote and curiously scrolled to The Weather Channel. The meteorologist was talking about a weather system in the Atlantic that had quickly become a tropical depression and was expected to come ashore on the Florida coast by the next day. Having lived in Houston for many years I was quite use to this type of weather, even so, I know that this type of storm is nothing to take lightly. There was something more intense about the energy of this particular storm that I could not put my finger on just yet. As I usually do in a case like this, I put forth a prayer for the intensity of the storm to be lessened and focused on the people in the path of the storm to have grace and protection, in the highest good.

Once this storm, famously named Katrina, crossed over the Florida peninsula the meteorologists predicted that it would reach water again in the Gulf of Mexico and head due north making landfall in Florida's panhandle. A deep knowing inside me could not accept their forecast. I knew that once the storm hit water again it would instead head west and make a curve to the north.

The knowingness I felt continued to communicate that the path of this hurricane would go as far as Louisiana and Mississippi where it would make landfall again. I felt a sense of urgency around this awareness and put out another prayer for Divine intervention.

My husband's parents live in New Orleans, and I knew there was a chance that they would be affected. I talked about The Weather Channel's forecast with my husband Robert, letting him know about the strong feeling I had of a different path for the storm, which would mean that there was a pretty good chance that our loved ones would need to evacuate New Orleans and come to Houston to ride out the storm.

A couple of days later it became clear that Katrina would not make landfall in the panhandle of Florida. Meteorologists would now be preparing the people of Louisiana and Mississippi for a major hurricane. Plans were underway to bring our relatives to Houston and more prayers were pouring forth for the people who would remain. As Katrina got closer to land, the city of New Orleans was in massive preparation mode. The reports of shelter plans for people who would need to leave their homes dominated the newscasts. One of the places that would be available for shelter was the Superdome in New Orleans. Video footage showed crowds of people forming long lines outside that facility to take refuge throughout the day and night.

I closed my eyes for a moment to tune inward to see if the Superdome would truly be a safe refuge for the people. I had major concerns for them. I could "see" in my inner vision, that they would be safe from the hurricane; however, I had a strong sense that it was going to be an extremely challenging experience for many of them. The inner vision also showed me a futuristic picture, more like a video, of the Superdome; I could see a section of the outer layer of the roof flapping loosely in the strong winds; the dome would indeed make it through the hurricane; however, I knew there would be enough roof damage to cause substantial water leaks.

The center of Katrina hit southeast of New Orleans on August 29, 2005. Winds downtown were reported to be in the category 3 range. Hearts from around the world watched and waited for the news of the fate of the people in the path of the storm in Louisiana and Mississippi. As I had seen in my earlier vision, the Superdome sustained significant damage, including two sections of the roof that were compromised; the dome's waterproof membrane had essentially been peeled off.

Hurricane Katrina will be etched in the hearts and minds of people around the world for a long time. The stories that would be told in the aftermath of the storm were from a wide range of experiences; anywhere from ominous to the miraculous. Many who remained in their homes had to swim for their lives, wade through deep water, or remain trapped in their attics or on their rooftops.

There were countless people who evacuated Louisiana before the hurricane hit landfall; a large majority of them traveled to Houston. After the storm, on August 31, conditions worsened in New Orleans and flood waters continued to rise from the broken levees. Governor Blanco of Louisiana ordered that all of New Orleans, including the Superdome, be evacuated. FEMA had announced that; in conjunction with Greyhound, the National Guard, 68 school buses, and numerous Houston Metro buses; the 25,000 people at the Superdome would be relocated across state lines to the Houston Astrodome in Texas. Roughly 475 buses were promised by FEMA to ferry evacuees. The entire evacuation was expected to take two days. By September 4, the Superdome had been completely evacuated.

In addition to the Astrodome, there were people in Houston who opened their homes to people they had never met before just to help out. Churches made arrangements to help in as many ways as they could as well. Monetary donations were coming in from everywhere to help with the enormous expenses involved. The efforts that went into the situation were momentous. Groups and individuals rallied to support the new arrivals in a myriad of ways. I knew that the hardships the people had endured would need to be addressed on all levels.

Several weeks before the arrival of Hurricane Katrina, I offered to help my friends Elizabeth and William take care of their family of dogs and cat at their home in the country near Austin. They had plans to be away on a trip for two weeks. I was scheduled to be at their home the day after the people from New Orleans would be arriving in Houston. As much as I wanted to stay in Houston and help out at the Astrodome, I could not let Elizabeth and William down. There was not enough time to find` someone else to take care of their home and pets while they were gone. My donations and prayers would be my best offerings to the new and temporary residents at the Astrodome.

Once I was settled-in at my friend's home I made it a point to focus extra time in prayer and meditation. I visualized the Angelic realm filling the Astrodome with Divine Light to support the people there in healing their hearts, minds, bodies, and Spirits, while asking for a calm, nurturing, and comfortable environment for them to rest in. A silent inner message began to surface; the voice said "Before you 'catch your breath' there will be another."

"What … Another?" I answered back almost stunned. I waited a few moments to see if there would be more to the message. I wanted to get more clarity and asked if this meant there would be another hurricane hitting Louisiana and Mississippi. It seemed like a long time had passed in the silence when I realized that I received all that I needed to know for the time being. I trusted that if there was anything else that my guidance wanted to offer it would come through when needed.

I returned to Houston just in time to be greeted with the news that there was a new tropical storm in the Atlantic. Less than a day after forming, the depression became the 17th tropical storm of the season on September 18, 2005, and was named Rita. A mandatory evacuation was ordered for the entire Florida Keys. As Rita entered the warm waters of the Gulf, rapid intensification began. This time the meteorologists had their sites set on Texas for potential landfall.

Rita became a slow moving hurricane and continued to gain strength unabated. On the heels of Hurricane Katrina the entire coastline of Texas and Louisiana were on high alert for another big storm. Once the meteorologists pinned a more precise prediction for landfall, Houston would be the prime target. It also meant the island of Galveston was in the direct path as well. You can imagine the immense tension that was growing after what had been witnessed from the devastation wrought by Katrina. It had only been a couple of weeks since the people of New Orleans had arrived and now there was a high probability that there would be another major storm to contend with, this time in Houston, which is only 50 miles from the coast, and the fourth largest city in the U.S.

By the time Rita got close to the center of the Gulf she became a category 3 Hurricane. The sheer size of the storm was larger than

Hurricane Katrina. Many Houstonians, and people from surrounding cities, began making plans to evacuate. It was now time for me and my husband to either start packing to leave town or decide to stay and batten down the hatches. I did not want to get caught up in a frenzied decision. I knew that inspired solutions dwell in the calm center of the heart space and a calm mind not engaged in agitation. In order to be connected with inner guidance in a way that I felt was most trusted I would first turn to prayer and meditation.

And turn I did. After moving into a deep silent space there were two requests for guidance that I had; I asked if Hurricane Rita would indeed hit Houston, and I asked if it was in our highest and best good to evacuate the city. As I waited in the silence I could feel my heart open and began to experience a loving presence within and beside me. The words "You will be safe" rose from that loving presence, powerfully strong, yet silent as a whisper. That was all I needed to know to prepare us for whatever might happen. I gave thanks with an immensely grateful heart.

For those who say "but I don't get messages like you do, that wouldn't work for me," I would like to share a few thoughts.

Even if you do not believe that you receive an inner voice or picture messages, go within anyway. Setting the intent in a silent still space will draw the energy to connect with you, even if it comes in a different form, or at a later time. It might show up in ways you are not even conscious of, yet the outcome will be much more positive for you than if you had not gone within for answers. There may be times when it feels less noticeable to you; there will also be times when it feels abundantly noticeable. When an idea comes into your mind, place the idea in your heart and see how it feels. If it resonates with you, then you will know it is an idea that will help you along your path. Remember to stay centered in your heart and take time out for quiet retreats at regular intervals. Whether brief or long periods of time, all meditation is good.

When my husband got home from work, I shared the message that I received earlier in the day with him. We both agreed that we would remain in the city and begin to implement our preparedness plan. We already had an Emergency Preparedness Kit, also known as a 72 Hour Kit, tucked away for just such emergencies. The items in the kit covered an array of supplies; flashlights with extra batteries, a hand cranked/battery operated radio, candles, waterproof matches, a first-aid kit, masking and duct tape, a Katadyn water filter and purification tablets, and packaged freeze dried foods, just to name a few items.

I learned early on, after spending many years living near a hurricane prone coastline, to have an emergency kit already put together before an emergency strikes. Everyone's list will vary slightly, depending upon experience and lifestyle, climate, and season. The level of comfort one might know when facing even the most trying situations, like a devastating hurricane, earthquake, fire, blizzard, etc., in part, can be measured by how prepared one is for those circumstances. There are many books on the topic of emergency preparedness, and there are some very informative websites that help educate the public; for example, Ready.gov and RedCross.org.

There are those who will tell you that you are in "fear and judgment" if you are putting energy into having a preparedness kit and plan. Simple caution and observation are healthy, and have proven the old adage "an ounce of prevention is worth a pound of cure." In more cases than not, many people have been grateful for the fruits that their efforts brought forth in time of need.

As our climate continues to shift and change, preparedness levels will rise to meet the needs that come out of that change. What I have mentioned here is very basic and for short term situations. In some cases, there could be even longer lasting effects to consider and prepare for.

There were other things that we were going to need to take care of before the storm would hit. We each needed to get our gas tanks filled, fill the water jugs that we had set aside for this type of occasion, at least 2 gallons a day per person for at least 3 days. We also needed to bring our potted plants and patio chairs indoors, and tape our windows with masking tape. There are people who would disagree with taping your windows, I have heard both sides of the debate; I felt that it was best not to "leave caution to the wind" and tape the windows just in case. Our pantry is always stocked with extra canned goods and staples; however I knew having a few extra fresh items on hand, like a couple loaves of bread, whole wheat crackers, nuts, and other non perishables would be good to have on hand as well.

As my husband and I drove to the grocery store we witnessed the long lines of cars where people were waiting to fill their tanks at the gas stations. Traffic was exceptionally heavy everywhere and the whole city was a bustle. When we arrived at the store it was no surprise to us that most of the shelves were already empty. We were grateful that we were not in need of most of the items that a lot of people came for since we already had those things tucked away in our emergency kit and pantry at home.

I was able to pick up one of the last loaves of bread available, a package of Melba toast, and a bag of dry food for our cat Snow. Some of the people waiting to check out had tired looks on their faces, others just carried the rushed energy about them, but over all, people were being courteous toward one another, as if the awareness that we were all in this together took precedence over the circumstances. Even the cashiers seemed to carry a sense of service about them much more heightened than I had seen before.

On our way out of the store we ran into a couple that we knew, Tess and Ron, from our condominium project. They asked if we were getting ready to leave town and were surprised when we told them that we would be staying. Tess mentioned that she had relatives in San Antonio, Texas and would be leaving first thing in the morning. I could tell that they were concerned about us, and I did my best to assure them that we would be all right.

We spent the rest of the day readying our home and supplies. I kept The Weather Channel on in the background, giving the TV a glance periodically for updates. When I heard Jim Cantore announce that Rita was now a category 4 hurricane, I knew that the energy people were already feeling about this storm was going to become even more intense. I stopped to take in the rest of the weather report, and then I shut the TV off. I felt I needed a break, and decided to have some quiet time. I rested on the couch only for a few minutes when the awareness hit me that the storm would continue to grow in speed, and would exceed a category 5.

This was startling, a category 5 hurricane, as far as I knew, was the largest category history had ever reported. Not that I was questioning the inner guidance that came, but I was shocked at the idea of a storm exceeding a category 5.

I had already spoken with our family members in Houston, and everyone was busy either getting ready for the storm or evacuating. I checked in with as many of our friends as possible, most of them were already on the road, some about to leave, and one friend, Dan, was still undecided. I told him if he needed anything just give us a call, we had plenty of supplies on hand to share. There were still a few more things to take care of around our home so I decided to wrap up as much as I could before it got late. I knew it would be important to get as much rest as possible to help keep the stress levels down and get to bed at a decent hour.

By late that afternoon the news was reporting Hurricane Rita as a massive category 5. When my husband got the news he showed great concern as he asked "Are you sure that staying here is going to be okay?" I could tell by the look on his face he was feeling quite unsettled. "I feel that what I was told, that we would be safe, is still true" I said sincerely. I gave him an embrace and said "You are my husband, and I love you, if you feel that we need to evacuate I will go with you wherever you feel we should go. We will be safe either way." He looked at me with thankful eyes and told me he was going to go meditate on it and would let me know what felt right to him. I was pleased to see that he was going to take the time to seek his own guidance from within.

Robert returned 20 minutes later and said "Okay, we're gonna hunker down here and wait out the storm." Whatever he had come to know in that short amount of time was enough to help him feel committed to his decision no matter how big the storm would become.

By evening, the winds were so strong that just four more miles per hour would make it a category 6; if there was such a thing. The news matched what I had gotten in the last inner message I received about Rita exceeding a category 5. Lt. Col. Warren Madden, a Hurricane Hunter and meteorologist for The Weather Channel, recorded a peak wind gust of 235 mph while flying in the eye of the storm, and called Rita the strongest storm he had ever been in.

Throughout the day and into the evening there was concerning news about the mass evacuations underway. The freeways and streets had become overwhelmed by the enormous and unprecedented number of people fleeing from the Houston area and coast line cities near by. An estimated 2.5 – 3.7 million people were en route to more inland destinations, making it the largest evacuation in United States' history.

Houston Mayor Bill White had urged residents to evacuate the city, telling residents, "Don't wait; the time for waiting is over," reminding residents of the disaster in New Orleans. After heavy traffic snarled roads leading out of town and gas shortages left numerous vehicles stranded, Mayor White had to retract his earlier statement with, "If you're not in the evacuation zone, follow the news," advising people to use common sense. However by 3:00 PM that afternoon, the freeway system in Houston was at a stand-still.

By late Thursday morning, September 22nd, the contra flow lanes had been ordered opened after officials determined that the state's highway system had become gridlocked. The Texas Department of Transportation was unprepared to execute such a large-scale evacuation. Coordination and implementation of a contra flow plan took 8 to 10 hours as inbound traffic was forced to exit. All the lanes on the I-10 Katy Freeway had been re-routed to head west only. It was like a scene from a movie; as far as anyone could see, there were lines of cars, both east and westbound lanes pointed in one single direction. Evacuees would wade through traffic Wednesday afternoon through mid-day Friday, moving only a fraction of the normal distance expected. Normally 4.5 hours travel to Dallas became 24–36 hours, travel times to Austin were 12–18 hours (normally 2.5 hours) and travel times to San Antonio were 10–16 hours, depending on the point of departure in Houston.

Many motorists were running out of gas, and some were experiencing breakdowns, in temperatures that were nearing

100°F. In fact, the entire region was affected by this heat wave. It was reported that many evacuees were periodically turning off their air conditioning to reduce fuel consumption. They were also drinking less water to conserve what they had, which can be quite dangerous in that heat. This would be the day that many would learn how truly fragile our complex modern society can be.

As these stories poured into the air waves, local citizens that had chosen to stay in town sprung into action. Stories were coming out that people were showing up on foot handing out bottled water to passengers in cars that were at a standstill on the freeways and highways. These dedicated compassionate people found ways to reach the motorists and share their resources.

The amazing community action by these individuals was a godsend to the people who had been sitting in one spot for hours on end. In some cases there were people bringing food, like protein bars, fruit, and nuts, to stranded motorists who were not expecting to be sitting on the road that long without nourishment. The enormous generosity of these angels reminded me of something I read in a preparedness book ... that when a disaster strikes in your area it will not be the Red Cross or FEMA, or the

Police or Fire departments, that will come to your rescue, it will be your neighbor. This is not to point criticism on government agencies. It is just that they will be so overwhelmed with the needs and events at hand that they could not possibly reach everyone who needs help in time, or in some cases, at all.

There were also stories of great hardship that would later surface. The Houston Chronicle would later report that the combination of severe gridlock and excessive heat led to 107 evacuation-related fatalities before the storm even arrived. According to local officials, the traffic reached a point where residents felt safer riding out the storm at home rather than being stuck in traffic when Rita struck.

My husband and I prayed together for the people on the roadways, asking for grace to make the journey a well supported and safe one. Especially for the children, the elderly, and those who had an illness, knowing that they would be the most vulnerable to the challenging conditions.

By now we were at our last hours before the storm would roll in to town. Most of the reports predicted it would be late into the night or the wee hours of the morning for landfall. I gave our friend Dan one more call to see if he decided to stay in town or had already left. He answered the phone saying "I'm still here." I love his sense of humor, especially in times like this. I chuckled for a moment and asked if there was anything he thought he might need. "Well I've run out of tape for my windows and I only have a few tea lights." I knew there was still time to get across town and bring him more tape and some candles, so Robert and I packed up the supplies and headed out the door. By this time the historic traffic that had been reported had finally made its way out of town.

On our way to Dan's apartment we felt like we were in an episode of the old TV show "Twilight Zone." The city almost looked like a ghost town; only one or two cars, here and there, where the streets would normally be a constant flow of vehicles. Trash fluttered in the wind on the empty sidewalks, and most of the businesses were already closed. It was a very surreal feeling for both of us.

When we arrived at our friend's apartment we offered to take him back to our home with us in case he would feel more comfortable being with friends. However he wanted to stay in his own space where he would be in his own surroundings. Dan offered to join with us in prayer for Divine protection through the storm, not only for ourselves, but for all areas that would be affected. I could tell that we were each grateful for the opportunity to share our hearts in this way by how deeply we felt the loving energy during the prayer.

When we got back to our neighborhood, while walking up the steps to the lobby of our condo, we noticed a man and woman we had never seen before walking down the sidewalk. As they approached us, without saying a word, the looks on our faces gave it all away. "Wow, we just about thought we were the only people left in Houston, are y'all stayin, if not you'd better get a move on cause that storm is expected to hit sometime tonight" said the man. "We're staying, looks like you are too" said Robert.

"Well I'm Tim and this is my wife Marta, if there is anything you need, let us know, we're in unit 114." There truly are no strangers in this world, especially during an impending major storm. This lovely couple, after meeting us for the first time, were offering their help if help was needed. I felt a warmness in my heart and smiled as I said "Thank you Tim, it's good to meet you and Marta. We're in unit 321; please do the same if there is anything you need. It looks like there aren't many of us staying so sticking together is very much appreciated."

Tim said "Sure will. Can you believe this quiet, I've never heard it so peaceful out here before, there's usually cars passing by all the time, people walking their dogs and carrying groceries in …feels kinda strange."

"We know what you mean" said Robert "it felt that way just driving around this morning." We each shook hands and gave each other a hearty smile as we said our good byes and wished each other luck.

As we walked in the door, Snow, our cat, greeted us in an unusually clingy way. No doubt he felt the change in the air and knew there was a big storm on its way. I picked him up holding him close to my heart. "No worries Snow" I said, "we've got you covered; there's plenty of cat food and water to last you a good while, and we'll make sure you're cozy and safe with us tonight." My husband gave Snow a gentle pet across his brow and a hearty scratch under his chin to reassure him as well.

By the time the storm reached our area, on September 24, it had been reduced to a Category 3 hurricane. It was the very early morning hours as we watched the storm roll in, about 2 or 3 AM. The pelting wind made for a pretty nervous kitty, so we sat him between us to calm him a bit. It was difficult to get any sleep with all the noise of wind and debris smashing around outside, we were a bit concerned that something could hit hard enough to break a window open. I reminded myself of the message I received that said "You will be safe" and relaxed a little more knowing that there would not be anything we could not handle that would come our way. Our prayers continued for all who might be in the path of the storm. We managed to doze off for a while once we got used to the sound of the storm, it was good to shift into a relaxed enough state to get some sleep.

Let not your senses deceive, for even as the tempest may howl, just beyond it lies a serenity that could not otherwise find you. The storm before the calm. ~ **Mike Dooley, a.k.a. "The Universe"**

By sunrise, the wind had settled quite a bit. We looked out the window and could see tree branches, leaves, and other objects strewn around the courtyard of our condominium complex. We inspected our windows and sliding glass door, everything was in one piece, nothing broken. The electricity had gone out, which was not surprising. We got out our crank/battery operated radio and tuned in to see how the rest of the city and coastlines fared during the storm.

In some areas, the effects of Hurricane Rita were not as severe as anticipated. We had gotten the clean side of the storm. The surge of the storm feared in Galveston and Houston struck farther east as Rita's center came ashore at the Louisiana border; winds blowing offshore in Texas actually flattened the surge, which was only seven feet. Still, storm surge of 17 feet struck southwestern Louisiana, coastal parishes experienced catastrophic damage; and the Industrial Canal in New Orleans was again flooded as the broken levees were breached once more.

We walked around outside to see if our neighbors' homes were okay. The swimming pool in the courtyard was filled with leaves and branches; aside from a lot of debris in yards and streets, everything appeared to be in one piece. There were a few places with downed power lines; phone lines were still operable for some areas of town. The family and friends that we were able to reach reported that they were fine; just a little sleep deprived from the howling winds and banging debris through the night. All were grateful that there had not been any flooding to contend with. A few hours later electricity was restored and the lines of communication were open for the rest of the city and loved ones to connect and share of their experiences.

Spirit of CommUnity

We are already one. But we imagine that we are not. And what we have to recover is our original unity. What we have to be is what we are. ~ **Thomas Merton**

I have had many thoughts about community over the years; what it really means and how it is expressed and experienced. I feel that it is as unique to each of us as we are unique in the world. Each of us has gifts of our uniqueness that we can choose to share with the world. As all gifts, the source is from the heart. This is why my own perception of community is that it is first of the Spirit. It is that place in us where our true oneness resides, and at any given moment, reaches out beyond the illusion of separation to awaken unity in unlimited and creative ways.

The day after the storm hit I heard back from my dear friend Debi. I called and left a message to see if they were able to reach their destination during their evacuation. She shared how her journey went while she and her husband Larry, their two collies, and her sister and husband, were traveling together from Houston to Fort Worth, Texas.

Debi explained that the day they started heading out of town, which was 2 days before the storm was expected to arrive, took nearly 12 hours to go 22 miles from their home in southwest Houston to the north part of Houston. They were traveling north on I-45 during the time that the freeways were gridlocked. No one knew how devastatingly packed solid the evacuation routes would be when they ventured out.

Tired and hungry, they decided to cross over the curb of the freeway to see if they could find a place to eat that might still be open. They came across a little Bar and Grill and stopped in to order some sandwiches. While taking their order, the owner Sarah introduced herself and asked what their plans were for the coming storm. Debi shared that she and her family, along with their two collies, Honey and Beau, were trying to make it to Fort Worth. It was hard pressed to find hotels out of town, near or far, that were not already booked up solid for the evacuees of Houston and other coastal cities. Even more challenging, it was hard to find a place where they could bring their dogs. Luckily they had reservations for a hotel in Fort Worth where they could bring their pets. They still had about 235 miles to go and wanted to know if there were any back roads that they could venture on to get further out of town.

Sarah gently said "You know that you're not going to make it out town in that traffic, and there are no back roads that will get you where you're going, much less find an open gas station that still has gas." Debi knew that Sarah was probably right and said that they would not be able to make it back home now that all of the freeways were open in only the outbound direction all over the city.

Without hesitation Sarah reached into her purse and pulled out a key; she put it in Debi's hand and said "This is the key to a two bedroom condo that I own, it's vacant and only a couple of blocks away. There are a few amenities to make you comfortable there. You take your family and doggies and go stay there until you're ready to head back home. Don't worry if it's a couple of days, just make sure you feel it's a good time to return. You can put the key under the mat when you leave."

Debi was shocked that someone would offer perfect strangers a home to stay in after only having a short conversation. Sarah could see that Debi was speechless and went on to say "I love collies too, and anyone who loves collies is a good person in my book."

"This is so kind of you, and you don't even know us. What can we pay you for staying in your condo?" Sarah would not even hear of it. She gave Debi a hug, told her to keep her money, and started writing down the directions to the condo. Debi sounded a little choked up as she got to this part of the story, and I was not too far behind. We both talked about how grateful we were for the wonderful miracles, no matter how large or small, that show up in our lives.

CommUnity Spirit is everywhere, sometimes subtle, sometimes huge and obvious. Look one way and it looks like there is not one friendly face in a crowd of people, turn around, and it is right in front of you smiling through the first person you see. It is within us all and comes out in some of the most surprising people and places. This is very important to remember as we go through the many changes that are up for us now.

Coming together in conscious ways to support individuals and communities will be one of the driving forces behind creating the new world that we all long for. It indeed starts with every heart. There were many stories of kindness that came out of the chaos of Hurricane Rita. There were also stories that were not so pleasant, due to the extremely stressful and challenging conditions that people were going through. Quite a few people experienced heat exhaustion and dehydration, anxieties were high and tempers were running short. The stories that are most remembered to this day are the ones that grew more harmony and unity among us, like Debi's story.

Spirituality is allowing compassion and love to flourish. When belongness begins, corruption ends. ~ **Sri Sri Ravi Shankar**

Where there are challenging issues, ranging anywhere from personal disputes to global conflicts, it will not change the energy that produced the conflicts if the people who have created them are held separate; meaning "us against them," or looked upon with disdain. It is useful to remember that they are still undergoing a shift in their awareness and understanding that all life is interconnected. Their actions that lead to challenges within the global community will change as their awareness continues to awaken. As each of us chooses to light a new vision of what our world can be, and hold them in the light of who they truly are, the world shines brighter.

Humanity is at a critical point in a process of transformation and needs the energy of love from each heart that is willing to offer it. There is a kinship, a natural flow to the Spirit of community, which is not only an act of "doing," or goal we work to achieve; it Is Us, it is a "beingness." It is consciously communing with the source of all that is, and all that is manifest from that.

The sharing of community Spirit is not only among those we are with at home, in our neighborhoods, workplaces, or churches; it is a creative expression of who we are among our unified experience of all life. Community (Come to Unity), or convergence, is with all energies whom we share this unified experience; all beings, all species, of all domains and dimensions - our animal, plant, and mineral kingdoms; all of the elements – water, fire, air, and beloved Earth; other planets, stars, light, sound; all are within the community of an even larger community of energies and beings, that we are all connected with.

There are no borders; only imagined separation. We each accept roles of stewardship within the domains we have chosen to have our physical experience in, and too, are aware that the stewardship is accountable for all the energy we put out into the Universe we live in. Understanding this will also help us to navigate through the huge changes that are underway. As Marshall McLuhan puts it "There are no passengers on Spaceship Earth. We are all crew."

Many have heard the expression that "we are the ones we have been waiting for." This is not just a cliché; all of humanity is rising up to create new paradigms where old structures once were. We are reaching deeper into ourselves and finding resiliency, united by love. I remember a few years ago asking Mother Mary how to see beyond the personal challenges that stood before me. It seemed that all I could see was a dense fog, I did not know where to start or how to move forward. She said to me "Take each step as it lights up before you." At that moment I could see, while steeped deep in fog, a light that lit up right in front of my feet. I stepped onto the lighted step and waited a moment; then another step lit up. I then understood that even while steeped in uncertainty, as we are willing to not give up, stay engaged with the knowing that a way or solution will come forth, a path will light up to guide us, sometimes one step at a time, and in some cases, leaps at a time.

We are artists designing our own new world. In a meditation I was shown the birth of that new world. It was like witnessing Earth/humanity as a flower bud made of brilliant light-energy that was blooming into a civilization of a whole new heavenly and unique world. I could still see a part of the physical world as the flower bud of light was blooming from the core of the Earth rising to the surface and spreading out, until the whole Earth was the full bloom of the flower. The sense that I had about the activation of this was like witnessing a beloved jewel in the crown of the Universe of many jewels – loved, loving, blessing, sending out nurturing energy and receiving nurturing energy.

In many ways we are going past our comfort zones and trusting the infinite wisdom that guides us. In the depths of our beings we sense there is a force of shifting currents that are nudging each of us to a level of brilliance beyond what we might have ever imagined before. Many of us are still exploring, through our hearts, what we want to change and what we feel we are being called to create. When I remember all this I have never felt better about the future and the possibilities that await us. We are adapting more and more each day, as we embrace change, trust that the wisdom within our hearts is vast, have confidence that we know more than we think we know, and remember that we are not alone in our adventure on this beautiful blue precious planet we call Earth.

* * *

Many of the messages that Mother Mary has shared are about the importance of truly connecting with our hearts and awakening to our Divine connection with all life. There is a knowing that goes beyond what we think we know … this knowing is deep, vast, and encompassing. In that "place" we experience a greater awareness of our Oneness. It is always there, always has been. Mary asks that we rest there, nurturing the awareness of that connection often. As we remember her words that were shared in the beginning of this book we are reminded of our Divinity and ability to rise like Eagles, far above any storm, and create anew …

132

Peace will stand. It will carry forth in humanity's efforts to aid the planet and help humanity. We must all remember that we are all One family under God who can choose to participate in the betterment of mankind and the quality of life. ~ **Mother Mary, Mother of Jesus**

About the Author

Claire Papin is a contributor to the books *Angel Tales, The Art of Manifesting,* and *When Ego Dies;* and has been a columnist for *Indigo Sun Magazine* with her *Joyful Earth Partnership* articles for nearly 6 years. Claire can be heard as the voice of Mother Mary in the best selling book made into audio *Mary's Message to the World* by Annie Kirkwood, and is the Marian visionary of *Mary's Lullaby* which can be heard on her website at LightedPaths.org. She is a pioneer in holistic media, and has hosted and produced the radio talk shows *It's All Good,* and *Wisdom Today* on the Wisdom Network, both of which aired coast to coast on *Sirius Satellite Radio.* She has also locally coordinated relief projects for children including *To Bosnia with Love* and *Shoes for Orphan Souls,* and has spoken for the *National Random Acts of Kindness Foundation.*

For more information about Claire, and to find the audio book version of *Mary's Miracles and Messages,* please visit her website at www.LightedPaths.org.

www.ingramcontent.com/pod-product-compliance
Lightning Source LLC
LaVergne TN
LVHW011240080426
835509LV00005B/564